MANTRA AND THE MODERN MAN

Author

PRABHA DUNEJA

Presented by

GEETA SOCIETY

2822 Camino Segura, Pleasanton, CA 94566, U.S.A.

Tel. : 925-484-5411; Fax : 925-417-5946

e-mail : duneja@aol.com

Website : www.holygeeta.com

ISBN : 81-7077-021-1
First Edition : Delhi, June, 1995
Second Edition : Delhi, April, 1999
Third Edition : Delhi, April, 2002
Fourth Edition : Delhi, Jan., 2005

Author :

PRABHA DUNEJA

2822 Camino Segura
Pleasanton, CA 94566, U.S.A.
Tel. : 925-484-5411; Fax : 925-417-5946
e-mail : duneja@aol.com
Website : www.holygeeta.com

Editorial:

Dr. Baldeo Sahai

Writer, Journalist and Fellow of Indian National Science Academy

Dr. Arun Mishra

Lecturer of Philosophy, University of Delhi

Publisher :

GOVINDRAM HASANAND

4408, Nai Sarak, Delhi-110 006 (INDIA)
Tel. : 91-11-23977216
e-mail : ajayarya@vsnl.com
Web : www.vedicbooks.com

Printed at :

RADHA PRESS

2465, Main Road, Kailash Nagar, Delhi-110031 (India)

Acknowledgements

I want to express my heartfelt gratitude to the holy sages of past and present and to other several scholars, philosophers and poets whose teachings and books have inspired me for writing this book.

I feel immensely indebted to my husband Amritji and our son Anshuman for their genuine encouragement and sincere support in the completion of this noble work. I am especially grateful to my respected grandparents Sri & Smt. Gangaramji, my parents Dr. & Mrs. Manohar Lalji and my uncle Prof. Nandlalji, who initiated me into the recitation of Gayatri Mantra at the early age of three. Also my gratitude goes to my respected cousin Mr. Rana Partap who had enthusiastically edited the first edition in June 1995 and also provided some valuable suggestions. I definitely feel thankful to Mr. Baldeo Sahai, a renowned scholar, to go through the pages of this book. A fellow of the Indian National Science Academy, member of Indian Information Service, a journalist, poet, art critic and author of several books, he has also been kind enough to give a Foreword to the volume.

—Prabha Duneja

ॐ नमो भगवते वासुदेवाय नमः

AUM NAMO BHAGWATE VASUDEVAYE NAMAH

YOURS TO YOU

"...Vasudeva sutam Devam
Kans Chanur mardanam
Devaki Parmanandam
Krsnam vande Jagatgurum..."

I salute to Lord Kṛṣṇa, the son of Vasūdeva, the destroyer of Kaṅsa and Chaṇura, the supreme bliss of Devaki and the teacher of the universe.

Invocation

Tvamakṣaraṁ paramaṁ veditavyaṁ
tvamaśya viśvasya paraṁ nidhānam
Tvamavyayaḥ śāśvatadharmagoptā
sanātanas tvaṁ puraṣo mato me

You are the imperishable, the Supreme Being, worthy to be known. You are the ultimate resort of the universe, you are the eternal guardian of the primordial Dharma (Righteousness). You are indeed the primordial Purusha, so I believe.

Tvamādidevaḥ puruṣaḥ purāṇas-
tvam asya viśvasya paraṁ nidhānam
Vettā'si vedyaṁ ca paraṁ ca dhāma
tvayā tataṁ viśvam anantarūpa

You are the Primal God, the most ancient Purusha and the ultimate resort of the universe. You are the knower, the knowable and the Supreme abode. The universe is pervaded by you, O'Lord of infinite forms.

Namaḥ purastād atha pṛṣṭhtas te
namo'stu te sarvata eva sarva
Anantavīryāmitvikramas tvaṁ
sarvaṁ samāpnoṣi tato'si sarvaḥ

Salutation to Thee in front and from behind, I salute You from all sides, O'infinite in might and infinite in prowess You encompass all, therefore You are all.

Pitāsi lokasya carācarasya
tvamasya pūjyaś ca gururgarīyān
Na tvatsamo'sty abhaydhikaḥ kuto'nyo
lokatraye'pyapratimaprabhāva

You are the Father of the world, moving and unmoving. You are the most venerable teacher (Guru) and highly adorable. There is no one equal to You in all the three worlds; how can there be any one greater than You. O'Lord of unequalled power.

Tasmāt praṇamya praṇidhāya kāyaṁ
prasādaye tvāmahamīśamīḍyam
Piteva putrasya sakheva sakhyuḥ
priyaḥ priyāyārhasi deva soḍhum

Therefore I prostrate before You and request for Your grace O'Lord. Bear with me. As a father to his son, a friend to his friend, a lover to his beloved.

—Srimad Bhagawad Geeta

Chapter - XI (18-38-40-43-44)

Reviews

In *Mantra and the Modern Man,* Prabha Duneja takes her readers on a spiritual odyssey through the depths of the human psyche to the esoteric truths that lead not only to the harmony of the innerself with society but ultimately to union with the Universal Self. Written with the same keen insight and poetic voice that makes her such a powerful speaker, Duneja's reflections remind us that while a *mantra,* as the distillation of Ultimate Reality, provides a doorway to liberation, it is up to each of us to walk through that door. This volume, like much of Duneja's other work, is immensely helpful for students who are seeking more than a preliminary understanding of concepts and theories—*Mantra and the Modern Man* beckons the heart and soul, as well as the mind. With a passion for teaching and her obvious gifts for speaking and writing, Prabha Duneja is fast-becoming an important voice among those interpreting Hindu spiritual practice.

—Dr. Norris W. Palmer, Ph.D.

Associate Professor of Religious Studies

Saint Mary's College of California, USA

Mantra and the Modern Man by Mrs. Prabha Duneja discusses the use of the mantra, or sound, as a path to the Divine. Repetition of a divine name has long been held in many religious traditions to be an efficacious method for the transformation of consciousness. Mrs. Duneja's well-researched work sheds much light on this subject. For those seriously interested in practical spiritual life, *Mantra and the Modern Man,* will be a very useful guide.

—Swami Prabuddhananda

Vedanta Society of Northern California.

The Lord has raised up in Prabha Duneja the skills and spirit of a great teacher. Mantra and the Modern Man is an inspired blend of theology and practice, inviting the reader deeper into union with the Divine. The combination of contemplation, active prayer, and discipline she teaches will bear good fruit in the lives of seekers from many traditions.

—The Rev. Carol L. Cook,

M.A., M.Div., Episcopal Priest, CA

In 'Mantra and the Modern Man' Prabha Duneja offers a simple and effective method of spiritual practice known as Mantra-Jap. By the constant repetition of a sacred word or phrase, spiritual seekers can learn to reorder their mental landscapes and, in effect, "pray without ceasing". (I Thess. 5:17)

For those who wish to deepen their spiritual life even in the midst of daily responsibilities of work and family, this book can be the doorway into a profound experience. The method can be adapted and adopted by a devout seeker of any faith tradition.

—The Rev. Lois F. Rose

United Church of Christ Great Barrington, MA

The entire universe is ruled by a universal law called *Rit*. This law becomes visible in the form of a vibration. The Great Philosophers refer to it as the Music of spheres. Indians call it *Anhat śabda, Omkar,* or simply Aum. Aum is the shortest and the most potent *mantra*. Everything we see is the gross condensation of A-U-M. The entire universe, say the *Upaniṣads,* has emerged out of Aum and shall dissolve into Aum. Going back to Aum is like viewing the process of creation in reverse—penetrating the gross till we become one with the all-pervading vibration. In achieving this objective *mantrajāp* can be of great help.

Prabha Duneja—a *mumukṣu* of great merit—had delved deep into the mystery of this sacred syllable.

She has also introduced the readers to a number of other *mantras* revolving round other divinities; each can choose a *mantra* which he loves most. It is for the first time that an eminent author has explained the science of *mantra* in a lucid language. For the uninitiated, it is a godsent opportunity to understand this esoteric wisdom and practice it to derive full benefit. The modern man, who is inclined towards materialism, is invited to test the efficacy of *mantrajāp*. If done with faith, he may be gradually elevated to a higher plane and experience hitherto unknown bliss.

—Dr. Baldeo Sahai

Fellow, Indian National Science Academy, Govt. of India

'Mantra and the Modern Man' emphasises upon the relevance of 'Mantra' to the modern living. The book is well documented and stresses the need of synthesis ancient with modern in order to achieve the perfection in one's life.

—Dr. Ravi Prakash Arya

Indian Foundation for Vedic Science Delhi (India)

There is a great wisdom in this modest volume. *Mantra and the Modern Man* provides a balm from the increasingly hectic pace of our times. At its heart, the book recommends not only a means of healing, but also a way of being in wholeness as part of all that is sacred. I am deeply grateful for what I found in these pages and can only add that Mrs. Duneja deserves a wide audience, indeed. ***—The Rev. Eric H. Meter***

President, Tri-Valley Interfaith Council

'Mantra and the Modern Man' attempts to bring about a clear understanding of the Universe as an Organic Whole. The author follows the path of devotion to God. She stresses the need of using the Mantra Technique to solve the problems faced by human beings and the environment as a whole. She has deep concern for serenity and coordination in the society. This book ushers a new intellectual movement for the present age and is a must for all, so that we can realize the role of 'surrender to God' as the most potent means for solving our problems. ***—A Reader***

One cannot help being impressed with the skill which Prabha uses in describing how Mantra can and should be used in bringing modern man into more intimate contact with our Divine Maker. She explains beautifully the benefits of doing so. Her broad understanding and personal experiences are amply supported with those of other distinguished spiritual leaders and teachers from many religions and from many regions of the world. Her use of scriptures from many sources adds authenticity to her work.

While I dare not claim to fully understand the depth of her writings, I sense a close similarity between them and many of my own Christian beliefs. Namely: Man's body is a temple of God and should be treated as such; that there is a spark of Divinity in all men which can only be enlarged as he draws nearer to God in thought and deed. ***—The Rev. Val Black***

Church of Jesus Christ of Latter Day Saints

Mantra and the Modern Man is a systematic presentation of quite beneficial self-training techniques for God-realization and Self-realization.

—Publisher, *Ancient Vedic Literature*

Mantra and the Modern Man enlightens the readers about the subtle understanding of Mantra and guides them into the practice of Mantra Jāp as explained in ancient religious traditions of the world.

Written in an accessible and informative style this book can help the readers to expand his awareness of the supreme self to which he should connect his life with, in order to understand his own spiritual nature and also to influence the life of others.

Focusing particularly upon the necessity of Mantra Jāp, this book provides the most appropriate guidance for living a harmonious life. ***—P.N. Bhargava***

A senior proof reader in The Hindustan Times

Mantra & The Modern Man is a spontaneous flow of scholarship and human sensitivity towards cosmos as an organic-whole is written under the frame-work which emphasizes the devotion for God. The author has forcefully stated how the problems pertaining to human behaviour and eco-system, can be solved with the help of Mantra-Jāp. Each and every chapter of the book shows her deep concern for peace and harmony in society. This book is an introduction to the most valuable psychological movement of modern age. I hope this book is read by every human being so that one can realize how does one's total submission in the supreme being can solve most of the problems.

—Dr. Arun Mishra

M.A., M.Phil., Ph.D.

Prof., Religion & Philosophy

Delhi University (INDIA)

Publisher's Note

'Mantra and the Modern Man' is the second revised edition of the scholarly work earlier brought out by the author Mrs. Prabha Duneja.

There is no question about the depth of spiritual experience, this book provides, from which people all over the world can learn in all respects. I definitely consider this book from the view point of religion, psychotherapy and metaphysics as one of the most valuable contribution in the field.

Her work combines the ancient teaching of the East with the contemporary thoughts and ideas of the West. It deals with the most traditional religious teachings known to the world. This is a systematic presentation of quite beneficial self-training techniques to enhance one's psychological, physical and spiritual horizon.

By *Mantra* the author means the sound energy of the holy syllables which forms connecting link to the cosmos as well as to the deepest mysteries of the Supreme Lord.

Man has three levels of consciousness, physical, psychological and spiritual. The author has been able to demonstrate quite confidently that the *'Mantra Jāp'* brings harmony at all the three levels of consciousness, electrifies the thoughts with spiritual power and brings an exemplary effect on man's thoughts, words and deeds.

The most significant aspect of Mrs. Prabha Duneja's work is that whatever she tells or writes, it comes right from the core of her heart, her own experiences and her own achievements in the path of God-Realisation. This greatly enhances the practical utility of the work *'Mantra and the Modern Man'*. In fact, every chapter of the book is so replete with author's own experiences, that the reader never gets bored at any step and as he proceeds, chapter after chapter, he finds himself more and more enlightened on the path of spiritual advancement.

Last, but not the least, Mrs. Prabha Duneja has been extremely gracious in listing some of the highly recommended *Mantras* for initiation and recitation. Each *'mantra'* has its own importance and special significance. It is only by contemplating and meditating on *Mantra* with faith, humility and devotion, that a true aspirant is able to understand the purport of the *'mantra'* in the right spirit; and if he is able to transcend it in his own life, the results are bound to be highly beneficial and rewarding. As Dr. S. Radhakrishnan puts it and the author quotes "every one of us is a potential candidate for the divine status". If *'mantra'* can help us in leading a good life and enjoy the kindness, blessings and grace of the Supreme Lord, it is worth trying.

—Govindram Hasanand

Publisher

Contents

Foreword

A *mantra* is like an atom of uranium, pulsating with enormous latent energy. This energy can be released when the devotee who repeatedly recites the *mantra,* becomes one with its vibrations. In the beginning of the creation when there was neither day nor night and nothing existed, totally windless, by itself, the One breathed. Those vibrations condensed in finer, and gradually in grosser forms. The forms acquired names and the world of numerous names and forms came into being. In *mantrajāp*—the repeated recitation of a mnemonic phrase—this process is reversed. Concentrating upon the meaning of the *mantra,* rising above names and forms, penetrating through the grosser vibrations, the person reaches the subtler spiritual realms of the One without a second.

Mantra is the abode of God, and helps in realizing Him. It is a special type of energy capsuled in the primordial sound of certain words, or letters. The *Vedās* say that in the beginning was Prajāpati, the Brahma, and the Word was verily the supreme Brahma. The *Ṛgveda* says that *Vāc,* the Word, is Brahma, enveloping the entire creation. According to a meditation given in the *Mūṅdaka Upaniṣad vāc viritascā Vedāh*—the *Vedas* are His speech. The same sentiment is repeated in the *Māndūkya Upaniṣad* which brings about a harmony between ourselves and the world. From the point of view of the *Upaniṣad* there is no unbridgeable gulf between the individual and the cosmos, the Jiva and Ishvara, the microcosm and macrocosm, the *Pinda* and *Brahmanda*. Through a *mantra* one can bridge the gap between the two. It is a link between the *Pinda* and *Brahmanda*. The Bible says: "In the beginning was the Word, and the Word was with God, and the Word was God."

Mantrajāp should be done by meditating upon the meaning of the *mantra*. Then the thoughts start taking the shape of the words and their meaning and help the intellect to flow into transcendental consciousness. In a state of superconsciousness, Indian philosophers have 'visualized' various *cakras* on the spinal cord, each having a specific shape, colour and letters. By special *mantrajāp* these *cakras* are stimulated, activated, and give supernatural powers to the person.

Prabha Duneja has immortalized herself by earlier writing a remarkable commentary on The Song Celestial—Srimad Bhagawad Geeta of Lord Kṛṣṇa. In that elaborate dissertation—*The Legacy of Yoga in Bhagawad Geeta*—she has proved Rudyard Kipling wrong and brought the East and West together by freely drawing from the philosophical font of both. By relating oriental philosophy with the thoughts of some western thinkers she has shown that at the pinnacle of the spiritual pyramid there is no plateau but only a point where all views converge into universal unity. Her commentary has been well received in India, America and Europe.

The popularity of her *Mantra & The Modern Man* is evident from the fact that so soon after publication, the book is going into the fourth edition. A *mantra,* she explains, contains inspired words revealed to Indian *rishis* in a state of transcendental consciousness. The *mantra* therefore has a spiritual aura and is imbued with powerful vibrations. By concentrating on the meaning of the *mantra* and repeating it over and over again, the person is enveloped by those vibrations which elevate and enlighten him. A *mantra* is a stepping-stone on the path of spiritual attainments.

When a *mantra,* says the author, is passed on to an aspirant by a realized soul at the initiation ceremony, it acquires a spiritual force. That force is drawn from the long lineage of the guru. But it does not make it incumbent on the devotee to physically serve the guru and support his theology or mission. A genuine guru is only interested in the spiritual advancement of his disciple and keeps in constant touch with him at the spiritual level.

Your *mantra*, Prabha explains, is your life-long companion, your most trusted friend. You can always invoke it in times of stress and strain and you are sure to feel relieved. The *mantra* also brings about a silent unfoldment of the aspirant's personality when he establishes perennial contact with *Sat-Cit-Ānanda*—truth, awareness and bliss—he is at perfect peace with himself, and therefore in harmony with the people around. *Mantrajāp,* if practised by the people, is therefore the easiest and the surest way, according to the author, to bring about peace on this distracted and disturbed planet.

The main cause for conflict in the world is that modern man is always running after sense-objects and is never satisfied. The more he acquires, the more he wants. He seeks satisfaction in the external world but the fact of the matter is that happiness lies within. If he has no faith in God, he has no faith in himself and in others. By *Mantrajāp,* his faith in God is restored and quest for happiness is internalized. To drive home her point, the author extensively quotes from great thinkers of the world.

Mantrajāp is an esoteric subject and there is very little literature on the topic. In dealing with various aspects of *mantra*, Prabha Duneja has rendered great service to mankind. She practises what she preaches, that makes her elucidation most reassuring to the reader.

—Baldeo Sahai

New Delhi *Fellow, Indian National Science Academy*

Introduction

Among ancient *Vedic* spiritual traditions, the most enriching, fulfilling, rewarding, and precious is the practice of *Mantra Jāp*. A tradition so rich in significance as that of *Mantra Jāp*, needs to be explained and understood by each new generation in relation to their contemporary life style. A *Mantra* is derived by Yaska from the word manana, which means "thinking" and by that the contemplation of God is attempted. It is a vehicle of spiritual illumination, in the form of self-realization and God-realization. *Mantra Jāp* is meant to uplift the life of an aspirant from the lower levels of ego-centric self to the loftier heights of Universal Self. It helps us to live in the light of pure awareness. It provides a new direction to our thoughts and channelizes them into more blissful and productive thinking. *Mantra Jāp* strengthens our unity with the Self. It is the most positive and beneficial instrument that can slowly bring all kinds of positive changes in our awareness. It helps in concentration and one-pointedness of our mind in meditation. It helps us to enjoy *sahaja avasthā* which is our birthright as human beings. In the words of Swami Vishnudeva Nanda: "A mantra is a mystical energy encased in a sound structure. Its vibrations directly affect the cakras or the energy centres of the body. It steadies the mind and leads to the stillness of meditation. A *Mantra* generates the creative force and bestows eternal Bliss. A *Mantra* when constantly repeated awakens the consciousness."

When we are in tune with *Mantra*, the whole universe around us becomes peaceful and friendly. In the words of Ellison Banks, "*Mantra*s formulated in the heart are true, not just because they capture the truth of some cosmological occurrence but because they themselves have participated, and continue to participate, in these same cosmological events." *Mantra Jāp* helps us to experience the essence of something which is real and yet waiting to be revealed to us; something so close to our heart yet which seems so far off. These words of Tagore also support the idea:

"...Open the inner door of the shrine,
light the candle, and let us meet there,
in silence before our God..."

This is how my *Mantra* came to me.

Ever since the day of initiation from my revered Guru, there has been a desire in me to share my experience of *Mantra Jāp* with other people. My *Mantra* is not just a sound, a syllable, or a set of words. It is a living reality for me. It is my best friend and the most reliable guide. Ever since it has started penetrating in the chambers of my heart I have had the feeling of undergoing a transformation everyday. The impurities, the fears, the insecurities are fading, and I feel more integrated and confident than ever before.

Although we can start our spiritual quest according to our choice with verbal prayer, bhajan and yajña but slowly we need something short and concise, brief but comprehensive in expression, which can envelop our entire thinking faculty, and the *Mantra* recitation does it.

As far as the superiority of *Mantra Jāp* over prayer is concerned, I strongly believe that *Mantra Jāp* is definitely more effective in calming thoughts. In prayer there remains a gap between I the worshipper and God the worshipped, whereas the *Mantra Jāp* bridges that gap. Prayer is an elementary method of spiritual communion. Prayer definitely purifies the *Antahkaran* (thinking faculty), but the method of *Mantra Jāp* is a very unique way of establishing unity with the inner self. It leads one from the gross to the subtle and to the subtlemost Self.

It brings total self-unfoldment and also gives us the strength to deal with it, because with *Mantra Jāp* we actually work in co-partnership with God. A remarkable role which *Mantra Jāp* can play in changing one's whole personality is something that cannot be described in words. It can only be captured with one's personal experience. With *Mantra Jāp* life in general becomes natural and easy. An overall ease envelops our whole personality. We feel lighter than before—as if tons of weight has been lifted off our shoulders. It opens the doorway to a very relaxed life style. Love, friendship, trust, and respect for others come naturally and our relationship with others starts improving. It brings inner peace and tranquillity—an experience of being at ease—*sahaja avasthā,* as described in our *Śāstras.*

At a time like now when there is so much restlessness of mind, when there is a decline in our ethics, moral values and self-respect, we definitely need something which can link us to where we belong—the source of peace, the God in us. Something that will bring spiritual awareness in our lives. Something that will give us strength and confidence in our attitudes; something that will fill the gap which exists between the lower self and the higher Self. The frustration in our behaviour is a reflection of our inner conflicts. So the call of the time is to deal with inner conflicts, the call of the time is to bring transformation at the individual level. It is there that the changes have to be brought about. I have no doubt that the solutions to most of our problems are within the reach of our own potentials and can be achieved with our own efforts. As James Allen writes: "Man is made or unmade by himself; in the armoury of thought he forges the weapons by which he destroys himself; he also fashions the tools with which he builds for himself heavenly mansions of joy, strength and peace. By the right choice and true application of thought, man ascends to the Divine Perfection; by the abuse and wrong application of thought, he descends below the level of the beast. Between these two extremes are all the grades of characters and man is their maker and master."

As the habit of introspection increases with *Mantra Jāp*, slowly the whole life inside is set in tune with everything around. We observe and experience that our life is passing through the various stages of self-development and enlightenment. As the Supreme Lord himself tells in Geetā :

"...sarvadvaresu dehe'smin
prakasa upajayate
jnanam yada tada vidyad
vivrddham sattvam iti uta..."

Enlightenment is indeed liberation and emancipation in all respects. Enlightenment is the world of peace and happiness.

I hope this small book will help the reader to expand his awareness of the Supreme-self to which he should connect his life, in order to realize his own spiritual nature and also to influence the life of others. Whatever one will read in this book may not be something new. All of us know these truths at the subtle levels of our consciousness; it only needs to be reminded again and again. In the words of Dr. Radhakrishnan: "Every one of us is a potential candidate for the divine status." Each and every one of us has the birthright to live a good life and enjoy the kindness, blessings, and grace of the Supreme Lord.

—PRABHA DUNEJA

"...Tilashu tailam dadhineev sapirapah srotah swarneesu chagnih Avamatmatmani grahteasau satyenainam tapaka yonupasyati..."

Just as the oil exists in the seasame seeds, butter stays hidden in the curd, water in the sediment of underground springs, fire in the wood, so the Supreme Divinity exists within one's Self and can be perceived and realized by true austerity and true knowledge of the Self.

—Śvetāśvatar Upaniṣad

"...Kurnnaveh karmani jijivishechchtam samah evnjvyi nanyathetoasti na karm lipyate nare..."

One with the Supreme Divinity, let every man resolve to live happily for a hundred years or more, with the gospel of selfless action and with an attitude of service.

—Iśa Upaniṣad

"Through birth and death, in this world or in others, whearever Thou leadest me it is Thou, the same, the one companion of my endless life who ever linkest my heart with bonds of joy to the unfamiliar. When one knows thee, then alien there is none, then no door is shut. Oh, grant me my prayer that I may never lose the bliss of thy touch of the one in the play of the many."

—Gitanjali

Rabindranath Tagore

Mantra

The word *Mantra* is a combination of two words *Man* and *Tra*. *Man* means the mind, our thinking faculty, and *Tra* means to emancipate. Our Śāstras describe it as *"Manan trayati iti Mantra"*, a word which emancipates the mind is *Mantra*. *"Mantra,* according to *Nārada Bhakti Sūtra* is derived by yaska from the word *Manan,* which means thinking, it is by which the contemplation of God is attempted". *Manan* a vehicle—elevates the mind to a spiritual concept of existence, and, helps it to settle in the supreme divinity. *Śruti Bhagawati* supports it in the following words :

"...Paranchi khani vyātra tranatra swayam, bhu sa tasmāt parag paśyati, nān taratmān kaśicat hīrā, pratyāgatmān mekśād averatā, cakśūr amratatvā michan..."

Instinctively our senses are accustomed to be *bahirmukhi*. They are in the habit of chasing sense objects. *Manan,* a continuous *Mantra Jāp,* brings a change in our thinking process. It persuades our thoughts to seek true happiness within our own self. It directs our attention towards our inner treasure, which is the ultimate source of peace and happiness. According to Swami Tapasyananda, "*Mantra* is something more than a prayer. It is in itself a word of power. It is a thought-movement vehicled in sound and words". He states that the meanings of *'Man'* and *'tra'* is 'to think' and 'to save' respectively.

Recitation of *Mantra* is indeed a vehicle of spiritual illumination. It helps the person to regulate, harmonize and bring the entire thinking faculty into a certain order. It gives the individual an ability to grasp the mystic reality through a very simple and effortless method.

There are some scholars, who believe that a *Mantra* is a word or a group of words, which expresses the concept of God and the universe. In almost all the scriptures of the world, it has been determined that it is the 'word' which has expressed itself in the world around us. In the 'word' lies the essence of the primordial sound, the eternal principle. For example; the first verse of the gospel of St. John says, "in the beginning was the Word, and the Word was with the God and the Word was God". While pointing out its similarities with *Ṛgveda,* Viswanathan quotes the following passages of the *Vedas*: "*Prajāpati vai idam agre āsīt* (In the beginning was Prajāpati, the Brahma), *Tasya vāg dvitīya āsīt* (with whom was the Word), *Vag vai parama Brahma* (and the Word was verily the Supreme Brahma)." The expression 'Word' used in the *Bible* is similar to the expression *Śabda Brahman* used in the *Vedas*. The *Sound,* the *Word* and *Mantra*—have originated from one and the same cosmic energy—The *Para Brahman*.

The *Upaniṣads* describe the primordial *vāc* (sound) in the following way: *Mantra* is a word of God, and, *Mantra* is God. *Yogasikhopaniṣad* observes *Mananāt traṇana caiv, madrapasyav bodhnath, Mantra mitucyate Brahma, Mad dhishtanato api va*... this means that both reciting and storing the impression belong to the same origin. *Mantra* is indeed the abode of God, and is also helpful in realizing God.

The notion of *vāc* is so important that the authors of *Ṛgveda* took its helps to explain the evolution of the world—vāc is Brahman. It is the *vāc* which envelops the entire creation. *Shri Guru Grantha Sahib* also explains the same concept—It is the *nām,* that holds the world, which is manifested in everything around. It is the *nām* that sustains all the three worlds.

A *Mantra* is the special type of energy enclosed in

the primordial sound. A *Mantra* may consist of a syllable, a single word or a verse. It is a concise prayer. *Mantra Jāp* means storing and restoring of a spiritual idea. Its recitation is like printing the impressions of certain spiritual words into the deepest layers of our consciousness. *Mantra Jāp* contains within its words a certain type of energy which replaces the old memory with the new one and brings a shift in awareness.

Regarding the source of *Mantras*, it is said that at the beginning of creation, some privileged souls were blessed with inner vision. In their deep contemplation, they heard some sounds and words which were called *Mantras*. With their spiritual experience they pointed out, that when our mind gets in tune with the inner *Nāda* (primordial sound) it can recognize the voice of the Self. The sounds which are heard in the state of inner unity are universal. They do not belong to any particular nationality, language, ritual or tradition.

The sounds heard in deep contemplation emerged from *Anahata Nāda* (primordial sound). The holy sages assimilated and recorded these sounds in their mind. Moving from less awareness to increased awareness, from gross diversity to subtle unity, they came to the conclusion that the primordial sound AUM is indeed the source of all the *Mantras*. *Vedas* are called the *Śruti*. Whatever was heard by sages in deep contemplation and meditation is *Śruti*. The *Mantras* are the sounds revealed to great seers and sages in yogic unity with the indwelling Para-Brahman. Thus, these *Mantras* are revelations. In the words of Andre Padoux, as he writes in his essay, *"Mantras—what are they?"* "Though Sanskrit texts describe *Mantras* as *sahaja*, this is not to say that they are spontaneous utterances but that they are forms of *vāc*, the divine word, innate in man, born of itself without external help, the word that reveals the highly organized, sophisticated form of poetic utterances, the *Veda*. All the letters of the Sanskrit alphabet, supposedly born in the Godhead, may be regarded as *Mantras*."

In *Vedic* scriptures, AUM is known as the *Bīja Mantra*. It is the original sound that envelopes the entire creation. *Taittreya Upaniṣad* describes, *"AUM iti Brahma, AUM iti idam sarvam"* which means AUM is the essence of everything around and everything is the manifestation of AUM. AUM is the supreme spirit. AUM is pervading in all this universe. According to Bhartrhari, a great scholar of India, "The *Mantra* AUM is identified as the root *Mantra* out of which all *Mantras* arise. This sacred syllable is held to have flashed forth into the heart of Brahama; while absorbed in deep meditation and to have given birth to *Vedas* which contain all knowledge." The same concept has been supported by *Māndūkya Upaniṣad*: *"Om ityetadaksharam idam sarvam, tasyopavyākhānam bhūtam bhavat bhaviṣyaditi sarvam Omkāra eva"*. "The holy syllable AUM is indeed the imperishable Brahman and the universe is the exposition of His glory. AUM is all what existed in the past, whatever exists now and whatever will exist in the future." AUM represents the sound energy of the universe. As pronounced, it starts from the back of the throat, fills the mouth and closes the lips with M. The fourth element is silence—silence out of which the sound emerges, which underlies it and into which it goes. Concentration on the sound of AUM opens the secret doorway in the heart centre and connects the individual to the indwelling Supreme-self. Also at the same time it connects one with the throbbing being that pervades the entire universe.

The philologists believe that all the vowels have originated from AUM, and have asserted strongly that if one concentrates and repeats the vowels for a few minutes, like A E I O U, the sound of AUM can be heard resonating clearly. The consonants are considered to be the images and reflections of the primordial sound. AUM is considered to be the source of all alphabets in Sanskrit and the source of all languages. In the words of Śrī Aurobindo, "AUM is the universal formulation of the energy of sound and speech, that which contains and sums up, synthesizes and releases, all the spiritual power and all the potentiality of *Vāc* and *Śabda*" According to *Māndūkya Upaniṣad,* AUM symbolizes the triads in time and space. The three syllables of AUM symbolize the three stages everybody goes through everyday. 'A' symbolizes the waking stage (conscious level), 'U' describes the sleeping stage and 'M' stands for dream stage. When written in Sanskrit, there is a curved line on the top which stands for dreamless sleep—deep sleep; when the individual-soul glides through the gap into the quietness of the Self. The dot on the curved line represents the Supreme Divinity in us. This stage is known as *turiya* in meditation which is beyond the three levels of consciousness.

Three syllables also personify the three stages of evolution in the universe. 'A' stands for *ādimātā* (beginning), 'U' stands for *utkarṣa* (sustenance) and 'M' stands for *mitti* (annihilation). It also describes *ākāra, ukāra* and *makāra*—combined together *omkāra*. This means that everything we see in the universe is going through an evolution. It comes into existence, it is sustained for a while and then it is annihilated. Everything is enclosed within the grasp of the swift moving time. Meditation on the holy syllable AUM enables one to get in touch with the various stages of consciousness and experience the reality of the world. The primordial sound of AUM is called *nāda*.

The entire creation has originated from the primordial word and the primordial sound. Each *Mantra* is a combination of some sounds derived from the primordial sound—AUM. The fifty Sanskrit alphabets and vowels of all other modern languages have originated from the primordial sound AUM.

Mantras of the vedas are meant for the entire mankind. *Vedas* means the knowledge of the Self, meant to be used and meditated upon by everyone. It presents cosmic unity. As Swami Satyasangananda Saraswati describes in the book *Light on the Guru and Disciple Relationship*, "The *Mantra* is a link between you and the cosmos, between you and the deeper mysteries of the universe. Its meaning is purely metaphysical and relates directly with the very core of your existence."

Mantra recitation takes us back to the source and renders peace and happiness in life. *Mantra* is a tool to achieve unity with the Self. In general, when we mention the word *Mantra*, it is considered to be some word of power only used for material gains and healing etc. It is looked upon as a mysterious combination of some syllables used for some hocus-pocus activities. By some it is considered to deal with black magic and sexo-yogic exercises. Usually the people mix up the words *Mantras, tantras* and *yantras*. Although *Tantras* and *Yantras* have been described in our ancient literature but the learned sages and saints usually do not discuss much about them. The goal of *Tantra* is very limited, generally selfish and usually related to the enjoyment of material and physical world. Most of the tantric rituals have been considered against the basic fundamentals of *Vedic* tradition. The ancient Sanskrit literary works provide some significant insights into the sources from which *tantras* have emerged. The *tantras* are written in a dialogue form, the language is very inferior and the style also awkward and non-systematic. There are some diagrams which explain how the *tantric* energy works. *Tantras* are magical and mystical in many ways. In general, everybody cannot make use of the *tantric* power. There are shrines and temples in India where people go to make use of the *tantras*. In those shrines the mystical power makes itself available. The utterance of the *tantras* is usually done with some special hand movements known as *mudrās* (postures). *Tantras* cannot be used by uninitiated and unqualified persons. It can be harmful. This is the reason that many saints don't even like to discuss about it.

Similarly, *yantras* are some sacred geometric diagrams used in astrology and in performing some specific rituals. *Yantras* are used practically for fulfilling worldly desires than for making any contact with the Supreme-Self for liberation. So *Mantra*s, *tantras* and *yantras* must not be confused to be as one and the same thing—these are different branches of knowledge.

*Mantra*s are a great gift of God to mankind, which originated with the creation. *Mantra*s have been written for the welfare of mankind. *Mantra*s are meant to connect us back to the creator to whom we belong, the voice of the Supreme-Self. The recitation of *Mantra* is reality of religion because it always brings peace and fulfilment. *Mantra*s don't belong to the Hindus only or just the people living in India. Since *Mantra*s are the voice of the Supreme-Self, they are meant to join the inner spirit of every single human being to its source. All of us belong to supreme spirit—the essence of life, the God in us. No matter, whatever the race or nationality, all of us are the privileged children of the God, pursuing one and the same goal in life; that is God realization and self-realization. So *Mantras* should be chanted and meditated upon with love and reverence, with faith and devotion. In the words of Śrī Aurobindo Ghosh, "The language of the *Veda* itself is *Śruti,* a rhythm not composed by the intellect but heard in meditation; a divine word that came vibrating out of the infinite to the inner audience of the man who had previously made himself fit for the impersonal knowledge."

Any particular *Mantra* which is given by a teacher to his disciple is known as *Guru Mantra.* In general, a *Guru Mantra* consists of one or more holy names of the Supreme Lord. AUM is usually included in the beginning of the sentence. This special *Mantra* becomes charged with a specific type of energy and brings some special blessings from the teacher. The spiritual teacher gives a new life to the disciple and also helps the aspirant to awaken his own inherent potentials.

"There was a door to which I found no key,
There was a veil past which I could not see,
Some little talk awhile of me and Thee,
There seemed—and then no more of Thee and me.
Thee in me who works behind,
I lifted my veil to find,
a lantern—amid the darkness,
And cried—it is Me in thee blind"

—Omar Khayyam

Mantra Jāp

The practice of reciting *Mantra* is called *Mantra Jāp*. There are some steps in learning *Mantra Jāp*. In the first stage one may whisper the *Mantra* as if saying something to one's ownself. The second stage is silent repetition with sealed lips and the third stage consists of simply reciting the *Mantra* in the mind. The quiet *"mānasic Jāp"* is the most effective and beneficial in all respects. The *Upaniṣads* and the *Manusmṛti* has supported the above statement with these words: the whispering *Mantra Jāp* is a thousand times more efficacious than the audible one and the quiet *mānsic Jāp* is one-hundred-thousand times more efficacious than the preceding ones. The *Mantra* should be quietly recited, repeated and remembered until it becomes a part of our breathing rhythm. Slowly, as we practise, it starts entering into the temple of our heart and glows like a gentle flame. Its recitation becomes effortless and starts moving with the rhythm of our heart beat—rejoicing the heart and delighting the mind. As it glows, it radiates through our entire being.

Some questions are often asked—Why the holy *Mantra Jāp* is so personal? Why so private? Why it is recommended that *Mantra Jāp* should be done quietly?

Mantra chanted out loud can disturb other people and can also bring criticism and discouragement from them. It can become a mere show-off and may expand our ego. As the ego expands, slowly the *Mantra* evaporates from the layers of the inner self. *Me* and *mine* becomes more powerful than *thou* and *thine.*

To quote the sage Angiras :

"Prachanani cha danani jnanam cha nirhkritam Jāpayni cha suguptani lesham phalam mamantakam."

Charity given in silence, knowledge acquired with humility and *Mantra Jāp* done in secrecy are infinitely potent in their rewards because it does not give any opportunity to our ego to get nourishment. *Smṛti* supports this concept as described in *Nārada Bhakti Sūtras* by Swami Tragisananda, *"If the reward of loud utterance is one unit, that of muttering to oneself is one hundreth units. Repeating in thought alone is one hundred thousand units."*

The loud *Mantra Jāp* is less effective and less beneficial because even if the tongue and lips are whispering the *Mantra*, the mind is occupied somewhere else. It's not always with us. That's why people who only do out-loud chanting usually do not attain much in life. In order to have a first-hand experience of the Supreme Truth, we must learn to live soaked in the nature of God and that is possible only with the help of a nonstop, quiet *Mantra Jāp.* With silent recitation, our thoughts are constantly hooked to God, so even when we are performing our daily work, it is performed bearing the presence of God in mind. Sages like Janaka performed all their worldly duties with their thoughts constantly anchored to the Supreme Self. Spiritual awakening dawns in our life primarily due to the grace of the Divine, but is made available to us through the blessings of the holy saints and by our own efforts.

Quiet *Mantra* recitation is more powerful because during the recitation, there is no loss of physical energy. If we are chanting out-loud, it becomes very tiring after a while. There is a tremendous loss of body energy which can be used for other useful services like educating and helping other people. Silent *Jāp* is a kind of internal dialogue and a potent weapon to establish the unity with the Supreme Self.

At the deeper level of consciousness, the

disturbances are far less than what we experience at the grosser level of our awareness. So the words of *Mantra*, and the thoughts which accompany the sound, are assimilated much faster. The intensity of sound increases as it quietly touches the very core of our heart. Ellison Banks Findly writes in this regard—"The power of the *Mantra*, then, depends not only upon well-tendered form, but also upon attunement with a metaphysical reality that, for the most part, is separate from man. This attunement, however, even though bespeaks a realm normally beyond man, is not brought about by a miraculous display of the Divine but by an internal searching in the body's own organ of insight, the heart."

Quiet *Mantra Jāp* strengthens the spirit of surrender, and the true grace of the Supreme Lord begins to pour. As the silent communication becomes stronger and stronger the spiritual energy of the individual begins to flow into the conscious states of mind. It awakens all the latent energies of the aspirant and connects the individual to the source of life.

Quiet *Mantra Jāp* heightens the aspirant's awareness and makes him or her more receptive to further learning. Quiet *Mantra Jāp* is indeed a foundation for advanced spiritual learning.

Quiet *Mantra Jāp* is a complete austerity in itself. It helps one to live in constant awareness of the Supreme and renders the higher awareness to aspirant, free of material and physical limitations. It keeps polishing our *antahkaraṇ* and as it mixes with the rhythm of our breath, it joins the rhythm of *anāhata nāda* (primordial sound).

Anāhata Nāda is the inner sound heard by an individual in meditation. *'Anāhat'*, as the word itself explains, means unstruck. At the *Anāhat cakra* vibrates a celestial sound which can be heard in deep meditation. When the meditator withdraws his attention from all other external sounds of the sensory organs, this celestial sound can be heard automatically. At the grossest level of consciousness the sound of *nāda* is more or less like the sound of humming bees—a little deeper, it can be heard more like the melody of a flute. The third sound is more like the far off ringing bells, and as the meditator dives deeper into the subtle layers of consciousness the *nāda* is heard like the sound of the celestial conch. Further, at the deeper levels of consciousness one hears the sound of *Viṇā* and then later the sound of drums which resembles to the thunder as heard in the sky before lightning. At the most subtlest level of this *cakra*, the individual hears the vibrating melody which resonates like the sound of AUM.

When the non-stop recitation of *Mantra Jāp* touches the sound of the long hum of AUM-M-M-M, the *Jāp* becomes effortless. It vibrates from the entire being. At this point, the mind remembers the *Mantra* and lets it go on as naturally as possible. It becomes a tool for relaxation, and to be at ease. Now, instead of reciting the *Mantra*, the individual listens to its words and sound. So, we can say that a beginner practises *Mantra Jāp* with concentration and efforts while an advanced aspirant simply remains aware of it. At the advanced stage of spiritual growth, *Mantra Jāp* goes on without any effort. Slowly this awareness becomes a part of our personality and stays with us no matter where we are and what we are doing. It is an experience that cannot be described in words. It is inexplicable and personal.

As the heart sings effortlessly the words of the *Mantra*, we feel as if the whole universe is singing with us. At this point, *Mantra* becomes endowed with enormous spiritual power, and as it circulates and vibrates throughout the whole body, it energizes each and every cell in the body. All the impurities are washed out and there comes a boundless love and devotion for God. The individual feels self-expansion in all directions—filled with boundless love. When the *Mantra* starts vibrating with *Anāhat Nāda,* the person doesn't need to perform any other ritual in spiritual pursuit. As described in our scriptures: *"...Sarve te Jāpa yajñasya narhatah shodashim kalam..."* meaning all the other rituals and external offerings that we perform would not constitute even one-sixteenth part of the ritual of inward worship which is quiet, silent *Mantra Jāp.*

Omar Khayyam has encapsulated the beauty of quietness in his following lines: *"All the secrets a wise heart has, Must be more hidden than the Phoenix is, Because concealment in the oyster-snail makes the pearl. From that water-drop that comes from the depths of the ocean."*

Mauna which literally means silence (stillness of speech) is a way of increasing the strength of mind. It is not only the silence of speech, but also the silence of mind. It refers to the direct control over thoughts in quantity, quality and direction. *Mauna* is an attunement with the metaphysical reality from where the flow of life receives its guidance and direction. This attunement with the source of life reflects itself in a very miraculous way, into the day-to-day activities of the individual. It manifests the beauty and the equipoise of those silent levels of consciousness, where the disturbances are far less than what one experiences at the grosser levels of awareness. Gandhi's thesis on silence is worthy to note: "Experience has taught me that silence is a part of spiritual discipline of a votary of truth. Proneness to exaggerate, to suppress or modify the truth wittingly or unwittingly is a natural weakness of man, and silence is necessary in order to surmount it. Silence is both a physical and a spiritual necessity." He further writes, "I have observed the spiritual value of silence. The time when I could hold best communion with God, has been indeed during the time of silence (*Mauna vrata*)". *Mauna vrata* heightens awareness and makes one receptive to the inner knowledge of the Self. *Mauni* is the one who observes silence, it stands for the enlightened devotee who has a total control over his speech and mind.

In some school of *Mantra Yoga,* the aspirant is advised to practice *Mantra Jāp* by writing the words of *Mantra* on a piece of paper while reciting quietly. This is a very tough austerity but it prepares the individual for quick success in *Mantra Siddhi.* In this process of writing and reciting simultaneously, the words of *Mantra* are etched in the memory and are recorded in awareness. This is also a very useful method which prepares the individual for all kinds of spiritual progress.

"Uthishthat jagrat
prapya varanbodhataa,
kshurasya dhara nishita duratya,
durgam pathastat kavyo vadanti..."

Arise, awake and achieve which is yours, with the help of those who have experienced the truth; the wise proclaim that the path of God-realization is sharp like the edge of a razor and hard to step on.

—*Kathopniṣad*

"Where the mind is without fear and the head is held high;
Where knowledge is free;
Where the world has not been broken up into fragments by narrow domestic walls;
Where the words come out from the depth of truth;
Where the tireless striving stretches its arms towards perfection;
Where the clear stream of reason has not lost its way into the dreary desert sands of dead habit;
Where the mind is led forward by thee into ever-widening thought and action—
Into that heaven of freedom, my Father, let my country awake.

—Tagore *(Gitanjali)*

Mantra & Liberation

Quest for liberation is universal, it is so in spiritual journey. There comes a moment in everyone's life when a voice from inside demands freedom from restrictions and limitations. It longs for freedom in life. "Go Home" is the cry of a heart that feels suffocated in the bondage of the world. The joy of living in freedom is a human prerogative, but only the few can really achieve it; most of the time we don't even understand the real concept of freedom. We don't understand what real freedom means and how it can be achieved.

Freedom is not running away from the world. *Mukti* or *Mokṣa* is not departure from the world in space or in any other world. Liberation and absolute Bliss can be achieved in one's present life-time and also in the life hereafter. Lord Buddha, for example, attained his mukti in his own life-time. Similarly it is stated in Geetā that one may attain mukti in ones own life-time. Freedom is living in the awareness of the Divine, freedom is the acceptance of the self, freedom is living a life free from worldly desires, freedom is living in the nature of the Supreme-Soul.

Liberation is a state of mind which we can experienced whenever we are in unity with God. It is freedom from the continuous chattering which goes on in our mind. It is freedom from the ghosts of desires, fears, anger, greed, envy and latencies of this life and many previous lives.

At every step in life, the person's own hidden impulses indicate to him that he is being a slave of his own conditioned behaviour. There are times we do feel suffocated in our present circumstances and the bondage we have created around us. There are times when we want to make an escape. I have often heard people saying I want to jump out of my head. Most of us are weak and unable to get out of the unhappy situation. We feel trapped and helpless. We do not look at the cause of slavery and instead of looking for emancipation, we keep on knitting the web of helplessness around us. As a matter of fact, our slavery is because of our own ignorance and surely our freedom in life is due to our own enlightenment.

What is ignorance? Being uneducated or illiterate is not ignorance. Ignorance lies in our spiritual blindness. Our identification of happiness with the material world is ignorance. It is because of this spiritual blindness, primarily due to the concept of duality, the rope of bondage exists. For example, it is our identification with the ego that gives us the feeling of I and Mine. It deludes our vision and makes it very narrow and selfish. Ego yearns to win name and fame. For example, when everything goes our way and we achieve recognition, our ego expands—but if things don't move the way we want, we often blame others, sometimes even God. In a state of disappointment and frustration, our vision becomes very narrow and selfish. As Dr. Paul Brunton writes, "in delusions of the ego, and in its ignorance of true nature behind, that which expresses itself in the personal and vertical Pronoun 'I', are the source, both of the evil it does and the ignorance it shows. In its unchecked selfishness is mankind's worst advisor."

In order to overcome the pressure of ego, we can make some changes in our thought pattern with the help of *Mantra Jāp*. With the constant repetition of *Mantra Jāp*, our identification with God becomes firm and slowly our identification with ego starts fading. As soon as the iron curtain of ego is lifted we enter into the world where I and Mine is replaced by Thou and Thine. It is difficult but not impossible. It surely happens in due course of time. As we progress in spirituality and our *Mantra Jāp* strengthens, we watch the play of life as a silent witness to ups and downs, but we indeed feel free of the effects. As the Supreme Lord describes in *Bhagawad Geetā,* Chapter 14 (19): "*...na 'nyam gunebhyah kartaram, yada drasta 'nupasyati...*" which means as an aspirant becomes established in indwelling-Self, he watches the play of nature and its *gunās* as a silent witness.

I really like what John Blofield has written. He says: "complete negation of the ego, conscious union with the source of the being is a task so hard to accomplish within one life time that not a moment may be wasted; for if the opportunity is missed who knows how many life time must elapse before the condition needed for further progress are encountered." Similarly my grandfather used to sing a Bhajan, *"Is janam mein laut ker phir āyeṅge ki na āyenge, kar lījiye saudā dharma kā nahiṅ to pīchey pachtāyeṅge"* (इस जन्म में लौटकर फिर आयेंगे कि न आयेंगे, कर लीजिए सौदा धर्म का नहीं तो पीछे पछतायेंगे). It is not easy to replace the feeling of I and Mine with Thou and Thine, unless the constant repetition of the Divine's name takes hold of us. As the *Mantra* connects our thoughts to the Supreme-Self, it automatically disconnects our thoughts from the old dispositions.

It is noticed that in general people live in bondage because of their own self-imposed restrictions and limitations. For example, whenever somebody does a little favour to someone, he expects rewards in the form of appreciation and some words of thanks. This way, the person definitely restricts his happiness and lives upon the mercy of others. He depends upon other people's response for his personal satisfaction and happiness.

In this connection, Dale Carnegie relates a true incident in his famous book *How to stop worrying and start living*, "I recently met a businessman in Texas who was burned up with indignation. I was warned that he would tell me about it, within fifteen minutes after I met him. He did. The incident about which he was angry, had occurred eleven months earlier, but he was still burned up about it. He could not talk of anything else. He had given his thirty-four employees, ten thousand dollars as Christmas bonus—approximately three hundred dollars each—and no one had thanked him. "I am sorry," he complained bitterly, "that I ever gave them a penny!" In continuation of this incident he further writes, "Instead of wallowing in resentment and self-pity, he might have asked himself why he didn't get any appreciation. May be he had underpaid and over-worked his employees. May be they considered a Christmas bonus not a gift, but something they had earned. May be he was so critical and unapproachable that no one dared or cared to thank him. May be they felt he gave the bonus because most of the profits were going for taxes, anyway. May be this or may be that."

The truth is that actually no one has any control on what other people think, what their responses are going to be in a particular situation. These thoughts of expectations are the ghosts which haunt people day and night. These thoughts of resentment and bitterness usually destroy all the peace and happiness of life. These feelings of pain and resentment have caused a lot of torture to mankind throughout history. People live in self-torture and die in ignorance. That's why Śrī Kṛṣṇa repeats again and again in Bhagawad Geetā, "Your right is to perform your work only and not at all to its fruit; let not the fruit of action be your motive". The transcendent state of yogic unity is devoid of all types of conflicts and anxieties of results. Once the individual becomes settled in that realm with the help of *Mantra Jāp*, he automatically becomes free from all desires of acquisition, preservation, rewards, name and fame. In that state of realization the attitude of selfless action becomes a second nature to the individual. Since the false sense of selfish individualism is dissolved, the person works very effortlessly and graciously. In the consciousness of inner unity and enlightenment, the individual's life becomes contented and his activities become fulfilling and rewarding. The well known key to the door of bliss in life is to be established in the unity of indwelling Self and perform all work in the unity of Yoga. It brings about clarity of vision, and the awareness of working in a co-partnership with God. In the words of Maharishi Mahesh Yogi, "Yoga is the basis of integrated life, harmony of inner creative silence and outer action. A man can't remain balanced in loss and gain unless he is in a state of lasting contentment. Yoga is that eternal, balanced and never changing state of transcendental consciousness which sets the mind free to participate in activity without being involved in it." Skill in action manifests itself from the equipoise, tranquillity and placidity of mind, and the placidity of mind is possible only when the mind is settled in the Divine. The performance of work through unity in Yoga is indeed the key to perfection in work and freedom in life. Any one who performs work with unity in Yoga, he lives in freedom and attains the blissful state of immortality in due time.

So in order to feel the joy of freedom we have to rise above all expectations and limitations of name, fame and rewards. We have to rise above the false identifications and make our links with the Supreme-Self. When we start living in the awareness of God with the help of *Mantra* recitation, slowly our desires for rewards, name and fame fade away. Our identification with the Self opens many more pleasant channels of communication with other people. It brings us at ease with our own self. It helps and improves our dealings with others and we naturally become very loving and forgiving. For example, why some people find it so hard to forget and forgive, because they are at war with themselves. The harder they try to punish the other person the more deeply they hurt themselves. In some families, the vindictiveness goes on for several generations. Another reason why people cannot forgive others is because they do not possess the ability, the strength to forgive which comes from our permanent association with God.

Living in the nature of the Self does bring

transformation in our mental attitude and overall personality. I have seen many incredible transformations of these types in hundreds of people in my life time, consequently I no longer wonder at the changes. As Tagore also admits it in his 'Fruit Gathering': "*I sat alone in the corner of my house, thinking it too small for any stranger to come, but now with thy grace when the door is flung open, I feel there is room for the entire world.*" Forgiveness is a great gift of God. To forgive is to feel free like a cloud wandering in the open sky. A forgiving soul is indeed a liberated soul.

Similarly, trust and faith in other people also brings freedom in life. As we observe, most of us are constantly haunted by the ghosts of distrust and doubt. We do not trust others, because we don't trust ourselves. We don't trust ourselves, because we are weak and have lost faith in ourselves. Lack of faith in our own self is due to lack of faith in God. We are constantly knitting a web of self-doubt, self-rejection, guilt and fear around us, and ultimately we do feel imprisoned in this self-made web.

In modern materialistic societies, the number of suicides is increasing everyday. People feel suffocated and trapped, they wish to escape from their present circumstances. Most of these tragedies can be prevented if these people are guided into right channels with the help of prayers and faith in God. As one of the most well-known psychiatrist, Dr. Carl Gustav Jung writes in his *'Modern Man in Search of a Soul'*, "During the past thirty years, people from all the civilized countries of the earth have consulted me. I have treated many hundreds of patients. Among all my patients in the second half of their life—that is to say, over thirty-five—there has not been one whose problem in the last resort was not that of finding a religious outlook on life. It is safe to say that every one of them fell ill because he had lost that which the living religion of every age have given to their followers, and none of them has been really healed who did not regain his religious outlook." Millions of people all over the world have experienced this truth and I personally feel this statement to be very true. Faith in God is the key to happiness, peace and liberation. From faith in God comes faith in our ownselves, from faith in our ownselves comes the faith and trust in other people. This life can be enjoyable and worth-living only if we could learn to live in the consciousness of God who resides in our hearts.

The other well-known cause of bondage is the

identification of happiness with material things. Overwhelmed by various cravings and yearnings every individual feels trapped and helpless. There is a famous saying, *"chaha churhi chaandari atha neechan ki neech, yun to puran brahman thaa jo chaaha na hoti beech"*—"Every person is essentially Divine, but because of his intimacy with the worldly desires, he loses his conscious relationship with the inner Divinity". Pursuit of false values imprisons the individual soul.

There is an illustration given by Rabindranath Tagore where he writes about the embodied-soul, who feels imprisoned and bound: "Prisoner, tell me, who was it, that bound you?". "Prisoner, tell me who was it that wrought this unbreakable chain?" "It was I", said the prisoner, "who forged this chain very carefully. I thought my invincible power would hold the world captive leaving me in freedom, undisturbed. Thus, night and day, I worked at the chain with huge fires and cruel hard strokes. When at last the work was done and the links were complete and unbreakable, I found that it held me in its grip." This is what happens to most of the people in the world. The desires of worldly enjoyment are indeed the cause of imprisonment, bondage and slavery. People consider their luxuries to be their necessities and that is why they become trapped. In this context, Frank Capra has written in his famous book, *The Tao of Physics,* "The Second Noble Truth that deals with the cause of all suffering—*trishna,* the clinging, or grasping. It is the futile grasping of life based on a wrong point of view, which is called *avidya,* or ignorance, in Buddhist philosophy."

Worldly desires are indeed the major cause of human unhappiness and bondage. Śrī Kṛṣṇa has given a beautiful example in this context in the *Bhagawad Geetā* chapter two verse sixty-two and sixty-three:

dhyāyato viṣayān puṅsaḥ saṅgasteṣū'pajāyate
saṅgāt saṇjāyate kāmaḥ kāmāt krodho'bhijāyate
krodhād bhavati sammohaḥ sammohāt smṛtivibhramaḥ
smṛtibhraṅśād buddhināśo buddhināśāt praṇaśyati

—it means that the person infatuated by some worldly desires develops an attachment for them; the desire which remains unfulfilled, ensues infatuation and anger; anger creates confusion of memory and loss of reason; from loss of reason one perishes. This is the ladder of man's downfall as presented by Śrī Kṛṣṇa to Arjuna. The desire, when unfulfilled, surely becomes the cause of anger and violence. It is the desire of accumulating more than others, it is greed and envy that sets people against one another. As E.F. Schumacher writes, "A life which is devoted primarily to the pursuit of material ends, and to the neglect of the spiritual, sets man against man, and nation against nation. Man's needs are infinite and infinitude can be achieved only in the spiritual realm, never in the material. Man assuredly needs to rise above this humdrum 'world', the inner wisdom shows him the way to do it." The test of universal love is indeed the absence of greed and jealousy. Anybody who is able to resist the urges arising from the material world becomes liberated even in his life-time. According to Dr. Radhakrishnan, "*Mokṣa* or liberation is in the lifetime. Not something after death. It is an experience of the present, not a prophecy of the future, it is living in the spirit of God who is the foundation and power of life."

As we become more and more convinced about the presence of God in us which comes with constant recitation of *Mantra Jāp*, our identification of happiness with the material world starts vanishing. We start getting the message that perishable things cannot bring everlasting happiness to the imperishable-self. The reason is that they have a beginning and an end. The flow of fulfilment which emanates from our own unity with the indwelling-Self, fills our entire being. It gives self-satisfaction, contentment, fulfilment and above everything else, freedom. As Tagore writes, "By all means they try to hold me secure, those who love me in this world but it is opposite with thy love which is higher than theirs and thou keeps me free."

Once I was interviewed by a reporter from the church. He asked me three questions:

1) What is God for you?

2) What does God want from us?

3) What responses people should make to God?

My answer to the first question was, "the essence of life is God." I related my answer with a story from *Upaniṣads* where Yajñavalkya once asked a question to Janaka. O'King! what is the light by which a man lives? The King answered: it is the light of the sun by which a man lives. Yajñavalkya asked again: when there is no sunlight, what is the light by which a man lives? The King answered it is the light of the moon. Yajñavalkya asked further when there is no moonlight then what is the light by which a man lives? The King answered: 'O'Sage! it is the fire by which a man lights the candle and performs its activities'.

Yajñavalkya queried further: there are some blind

people who cannot see the candle light, can you tell me what is the light by which a man lives? The King answered: 'O'Sage! the sound guides him to find his way to perform his activities'. Yajñavalkya further said: O'King! there are people who are deaf and dumb. They have no concept of sound because they cannot hear. So what is the light by which such a man lives? To this the King answered: 'O' Sage! it is the light of the Self which guides a man to live'. It is indeed the light of the Self which is the essence of life and is the God in us. It is the light of the Self which guides man in all respects. It illumines the inner world and the outer world. It is the light which energizes every little molecule in the universe and every little cell in our body. This light is the inner intelligence, the Supreme Lord residing in our body and everywhere around. The same concept has been described in the *Geetā* in Chapter 13 (17): *"...jyotiṣāmapi tajjyotis tamasaḥ param ucyate jñānaṁ jñeyaṁ jñānagamyaṁ hṛdi sarvasya viṣṭhitam..."* This verse means that the Supreme Lord is the light of all lights and beyond darkness. He is knowledge, the object of knowledge, as well as the goal of knowledge. He is seated in the hearts of all.

My answer to the second question was that the

God wants us to live in unity with Him. The Supreme Self, *Paramātmā,* wants its fragment *Jīvātmā* to stay in touch with Him and to work in a co-partnership with Him.

The third question 'what responses people should make to God?' To that my answer was, we should offer all our work in service to God. This is what God wants from us. It is the total surrender that gives freedom to *Jīvātamā.* As the sage Vyāsa has written: *"...eko Mantras tasya namani yani, karma payekam tasya devasya seva..."* there is only one *Mantra* and that is the name of God; there is only one karma and that is the service to God. It is indeed the attitude of service to the Supreme Divinity which gives freedom in life.

Those who are liberated in their life-time, their status is that of *jīvan mukta.* They live in the world like anybody else, but their activities are centred in God. Their appearance doesn't change but *Jīvātmā* who resides in the body is slowly liberated from its false identifications. *Jīvātmā* transcends all limitations and feels free with the repetition of *Mantra.*

The Soul (*ātmā*) is pure, lucid and self-illuminated. When the Soul identifies itself with the body and the three *guṇas* of nature then it is designated as *Jīvātmā* (embodied Soul). This nescience is the cause of bondage from birth to birth. *Jīvātmā* (embodied Soul) forgets its true nature. But with the help of constant *Mantra Jāp*—i.e. calling upon the name of God, realization of the Self beyond body and the three *guṇas* is realized and *Jīvātmā* transcends to its essential unconditioned nature. From *Jīvātmā* it becomes *mahātmā* and gradually *Paramātmā* (A liberated Soul). In the words of my revered uncle Professor Nandlalji, "*Na mein deha, na deha ke dharmā, na mein prāṇ na indrya karmā, na mein mana budhi, cit ahaṅkārā guṇātīta mein in se nyārā.*" (न मैं देह, न देह के धर्मा, न मैं प्राण न इन्द्रियः कर्मा, न मैं मन बुद्धि चित अहंकारा गुनातीत मैं इन से न्यारा).

To live in this enlightened consciousness is indeed living in eternity and total bliss. A liberated soul looks at every thing from a different perspective. He doesn't get puffed up at his own state of being illuminated and doesn't worry if he is not rewarded for his virtuous deeds. Since such a person always lives in unity with the Indwelling-Self, he feels very secure, confident and makes very quick and firm decisions. All of his dealings come from the purity of his heart. His constant identity with the Supreme gives him the strength to rise above the dualities of life. He regards pleasure and pain, loss and gain, honour and dishonour as passing phases of life. He looks at them as the appearance and disappearance of kaleidoscopic dispositions. He beholds the tragedies and comedies of this ever changing world with an attitude of unflinching happiness. He is always serene, tranquil and free.

This reminds me of an incident mentioned by Christopher Isherwood in *'The Life Story of Rāma-kṛṣṇa'*. He writes that "one time Rāmakṛṣṇa, who was a chief priest at the Kali temple, Calcutta, made some mistakes during the Durga Pooja. The managing committee of the temple decided to get rid of him. Accordingly, one of the temple officials came to Śrī Rāmakṛṣṇa and ordered him to leave at once. Without the least resentment or dismay Rāmakṛṣṇa picked up his towel, slung it over his shoulder and walked unprotestingly out of the room which had been his home for the last 26 years. He had almost reached the gate of the compound when people came running after him crying, "Please stay! We beg you to stay!" At this, Rāmakṛṣṇa smiled, turned around without saying a word, went back to his room, sat down and continued the conversation he had been having with some devotees, as if nothing unusual had happened." This is what we call *Gunatitah ca ucyate*, or the freedom of *Jīvātmā* in one's life-time. Total absence of ego, perfect calmness, self-mastery and righteous actions, characterize the lives of the liberated saints.

After achieving this state of liberation, it is a matter of personal choice whether one takes an active interest in the world, or totally renounces the world. For example, the Rishi Yajñavalkya renounced the world to live in the forest whereas the king Janaka ruled his empire. Where to live and what to do is immaterial for the soul who has realized the God. All of his activities are centred around the Supreme-Self, and all of his work is offered as a service to God. King Janaka lived as an embodiment of the Divine. He has been called *Vedehi*. This means that he always lived soaked in the nature of the Divine. He looked at his body just as a frame and a vehicle to perform the worldly activities.

To be liberated and emancipated is to rise above the dualities and conflicting emotions of life. It is to be free and integrated. The conditioned behaviour which is irrelevant and inappropriate gets eliminated. A liberated individual is happy, contented and illuminated. He has the ability to peel away the unpleasant past and he holds the courage to live with the situation at hand.

Since he lives in harmony with his body, he knows how to listen to its silent moods and how to deal with each one of them. A liberated individual is a good listener. His mind, inner-self and body work in a unison. Everything he speaks comes from the depth of his heart. Truth, fearlessness, honesty and sincerity radiate from him. A person settled in the integrity of the inner wisdom, has the courage to take responsibility for his decisions. He never feels ashamed and hardly blames others for his failures. This is the meaning of living in freedom and liberation.

The constant repetition of *Mantra* brings a new direction to our lives and eventually liberates us in all respects. It works at our sub-conscious level and gradually brings some dramatic changes in our day-to-day life. Slowly and gradually a new person emerges from old one with the help of *Mantra Jāp*—the type of person we always aspired for.

Sometimes people expect these changes to occur overnight. I remember people losing their faith in *Mantra* out of frustration. As I said earlier that each one of us is different from the others, for the way we think and believe, so the effects of *Mantra* also vary from individuals to individuals. To some people the transformation occurs within a few days. For some it may take few months and for some it takes years. It all depends upon receptiveness and the thirst for the eternal Bliss. As Swāmi Rāmakṛṣṇa has said: "Out of the myriads of paper kites that are seen flying in the air, only one or two get free by the snapping of the string. So out of hundreds of aspirants practising spiritual discipline only one or two get free from worldly bondage." The reason is that only a few of us truly learn to love God, trust God, and learn to surrender in God with acceptance, willingness and faith.

The undisputed truth is that constant recitation of *Mantra* does bring changes in our personalities over a period of time. As we notice, the changes in our physical looks occur very slowly and often unnoticeably. We look at ourselves everyday in the mirror and hardly notice any particular change. But if we compare our photograph which was taken five years ago with the one which is taken today, we will definitely see a lot of changes. In our day-to-day life we may not notice much change in our appearance but when we meet our friends after a long time, they can definitely point out to some changes in our looks. Change in our looks is a continuous process which goes on unnoticed. Similarly the changes in our attitude and behaviour do occur with *Mantra Jāp* but very slowly. Those become visible over a period of time and are indeed reflected in our day-to-day life. The freedom and liberation in life can be definitely achieved with the constant practice of *Mantra Jāp*. The *Nārada Bhakti Sūtra* describes, "As the oil poured from one vessel into another falls in an unbroken line; similarly when the mind thinks of the Supreme in unbroken stream of *Mantra Jāp*, definitely we move from ignorance to enlightenment, from unreal to real and from bondage to freedom.

"...Upjai Rāma caran viśvāsā bhavanidhi tara nara binhī prayāsā..."

"...उपजई राम चरन विश्वासा भवनिधि तर नर बिन्ही प्रयासा.."

—Rāmāyaṇa

[The Mantra of Victory over Death]

महामृत्युञ्जय-मन्त्र

ओं त्र्यम्बकं यजामहे सुगन्धिं पुष्टिवर्धनम्।
ऊर्वारुकमिव बन्धनात् मृत्योर्मुक्षीय माऽमृतात्॥

tryaṁbakaṁ yajāmahe
sugaṅdhiṁ puṣṭivardhanaṁ
ūrvārukmiva baṅdhanāt
mṛtyormukṣīya mā'mṛtāt.

—*Yajurveda 3.60*

The Great *Mahāmṛtyuñjaya mantra* is addressed to the indwelling Shiva for long healthy, wholesome life and liberation from the fear of death. The constant devoted repetition of this *mantra* connects the individual to the source of life and he is blessed with the experiential knowledge of his own immortality; which brings liberation from the fear of death and also the rich experience of being ageless, timeless and immortal.

The sound energy of the holy syllable AUM is indeed a connecting link to the cosmos as well as to the deepest mysteries of the Supreme-Self.

Mantra—A vehicle towards the goal in meditation

Meditation is a combination of two words, namely, Medi and Tation—Its meaning is to attend to the thoughts with attention and intention. It is one of the greatest arts. In meditation a person becomes introduced to his own self in all respects. While meditating an individual learns to attend, watch, observe and behold the movement of his thoughts, aspirations and dreams. It is one of the highest form of discipline which is cultivated with the practice of living in constant awareness of the Self.

In meditation-practice one monitors not only the quality of thoughts, but the quantity and the direction of thoughts as well. In the process of monitoring the thinking faculty, the person experiences for himself the majesty of the Indweller. The techniques which are used by the yogis, saints, seers, mystics and the householders do vary to some extent, but in general everyone follows similar guidelines. All the prescribed techniques are generally meant to induce a contemplative mood, that would assist the person for inner integration, peace and tranquillity. The key to success in meditation is the constant regular practice and the steadfastness in attitude. In meditation the individual learns to attend to the internal dialogue which goes on in mind incessantly. He educates himself in monitoring the movements of his thoughts and learns to direct them into the quietness of the Self. Success in meditation is indeed quite difficult, because occasionally the waves of thoughts surge and subside in a very disgusting manner. In the beginning, people become very frustrated and discouraged. The sages indicate that when effort in meditation is purely linked with the religious pursuit, and the goal of self-realization, then assistance for success comes from within.

The grace of Indweller is revealed in the daily meditation session and the person is guided into yogic unity in due time. The advanced meditators do experience the ecstatic trance, and occasionally enter into the state of unity with the Lord. The yogins derive deep satisfaction from such an experience. The subtle joy and exquisiteness of this union can only be understood by those who have really experienced it in their own self. Meditation is not just a religious practice, but it is certainly a necessity of life. It helps the individual to live in perfect harmony with his own innerself, and with others.

The goal of meditation is to be at ease with our own selves. It is a state of peace and tranquillity our scriptures call it *saheja avasthā.* Often it happens that a meditation period passes in vain with the mind behaving more like a monkey. Constant struggle is required to accomplish that which is absolutely effortless.

The Infinite Divinity cannot be perceived by the finite sense-organs. So in order to transcend the finitude and to remain constantly linked with the Infinite we have to train ourselves. With constant *Mantra Jāp* our mind gets into the habit of transcending the finite boundaries and rests in the Infinite Divinity. *Jāp* also helps our mind to form an idea of God. As the idea takes some form and shape, the concentration which is required in meditation is easily achieved. Osho writes in his book, *Meditation: the Art of Ecstasy,* "Meditation means surrender, total letting go. As soon as someone surrenders himself he finds himself in the hands of Divinity. If we cling to ourselves we cannot be one with Almighty. When the waves disappear, they become the ocean itself."

According to my own personal experience, *Mantra Jāp,* indeed, brings the spirit of total surrender. We cannot meditate on God simply by knowing the technique of meditation. The principal factor that enables us to concentrate on God is by living in constant unity with God. It is described in the teachings of Śrī Rāmakṛṣṇa that the magnetic needle points always to the north, hence the sailing vessel does not lose its course. So, as long as the heart of man is directed towards God, he cannot be lost in the ocean of worldliness. Persistent repetition of holy *Mantra* helps in purifying, cleansing and emptying the mind. This state is absolutely necessary for successful meditation. Repeating the name of God helps us to develop spiritual insight and intensifies our devotion to God, and longing for His vision. Relation between God and his name is natural.

Mantra has the power to awaken, within the mind the corresponding God consciousness, and it does prepare the mind for the goal. Through constant repetition the mind gets into the habit of being absorbed in the spiritual reality created by the *Mantra.* A very good example can be given from *Chāndogya Upaniṣad.* Dr. Radhakrishnan translates it in these words, "Just as a bird tied by a string, after flying in different far-off directions, when does not find a resting place anywhere else, settles down at last to the place where it is bound, exactly like that the mind after running in various directions without finding silence and peace anywhere else settles down in breath. The breath is the manifestation of the Supreme-Self—*Atman.* The word *Atman* has been derived from *An,* which means to breath. As described in *Ṛgveda, Atma te vatah*—Atman is the breath of life. So when the mind settles down into the breath it nestles in the Supreme Self."

In general, people consider *Mantra Jāp* a very inferior type of penance and fail to realize its strength and comprehensive power. They think that the most impressive spiritual disciplines are yoga, meditation, yajña and other tough penances. They definitely fail to realize the atomic power of the *Mantra Jāp* and don't pay much attention to it. Infact *Mantra Jāp* is the seed, the beginning, the nucleus around which one constructs the entire yogic and spiritual discipline. According to sage Patanjali, "Omkar is the manifesting word of Brahman. He assures that its repetition can stabilize our thoughts and helps us to settle in meditation."

We cannot meditate on God just by learning the techniques and technicalities of meditation. The most important factor which enables the meditator to be at ease, is his constant association with God, every minute of day-to-day life. It is the person's friendship with the Divine, living in constant association with the Divine which helps his meditation-session. In general we meditate upon those factors which are important to us. For example, we meditate upon our job, our son or wife or any other thing. Ninety nine per cent of our thoughts move around the person or the thing we love. So if we love some thing and meditate on something else, the meditation period goes in vain. It is indeed the cultivation of love and friendship of God which is more important before we actually start meditating on God. If we are in perpetual unity with the Divine while working in the office, while eating, talking or doing other things of daily life, the meditation on God will also come effortlessly. This habit can be well-cultivated with the help of *Mantra Jāp* with concentration on its meaning. As Emerson writes, "the key to every man is his thought. Sturdy and defying though he looks he has a helm he obeys, which is the idea after which all his facts are classified. He can only be reformed by showing him a new idea which commands his own."

In the path of spirituality, at beginning the seeker

conceives God as existing far away from him. But as he progresses in spiritual life with the help of the sacred word and primordial sound, he becomes more and more aware of an intimate relationship with the Supreme Being. The first experience of spirituality is: "*...twam ādidevaḥ puruṣaḥ purāṇaḥ, tvam asya visvasya param nidhānam, vetta si vedyam ca param ca dhama, tvaya tatam visvam anantarūpa...*" This means that thou art Prime Deity, the most ancient Person. Thou art the ultimate resort, the knower and the knowable. It is Thou by whom the universe is pervaded, O' One of infinite forms.

In the second stage of spirituality the relationship becomes very intimate and personal. For example, the devotee calls upon God as a dear friend, mother or father, *"twameva mata ca pita twameve, twameve bandhuḥ ca sakhā twameve"* In the third stage, the aspirant perceives the essentiality of the Divine and realizes himself being a spiritual entity, pure, luminous and free. *Tattvamasi*—I am Thou and Thou are I.

There is a story in our *Puranas* which describes this concept. Once Lord Rāma—the God-incarnate, asked his great devotee Hanuman, "O son tell me what type of relationship you hold for Me and how you meditate upon Me". Śrī Hanumāna replied "O' Rāma, sometime I look upon You as 'Purna', the undivided 'One, at other moment I look upon You as undivided but at the same time reflecting through everything and everybody. Then I look upon myself as a fragment of You. At other times, I contemplate upon You as my Divine master and think of myself as Your humble servant. When however I am blessed with inner unity and the experiential knowledge of the Self then I perceive that 'I am Thou' and 'Thou art I'—*Tattvamasi*".

Expansion of self can only be achieved by overcoming the limitations of the I and Mine. So, with the practice of *Mantra* as our identification with the ever luminous Self becomes firm, our identification with ego slowly fades away. The thinner is the curtain of ego, the easier it becomes to tear it in meditation. So repetition of the *Mantra*—which is a concentrated form of prayer—is indeed very closely linked with meditation. It is the spontaneous longing for the vision of the Supreme that can tune our thoughts and train the subtle layers of our mind. It is not a calculated devotion but a natural relationship. It is the nonstop *Jāp* which helps us to enjoy meditation. Meditation is the final spiritual course for enjoying unity with God, but until the mind is trained to stay absorbed in God, the Supreme Lord is not revealed.

Describing the power of *Mantra Jāp* as an important tool in meditation Swāmi Yatishwarananda writes in his book, *Meditation and Spiritual Life,* "In the beginning of spiritual life you need not bother about real meditation. Do *Jāp* and dwell on your *Ista Devata.* In due course *Jāp* will develop into *dhyana* which means unbroken thought on the theme for meditation like the unbroken current or flow of oil from one cup to another. Through *Jāp* the Divine spirit will become more real than the world. And only then will real *dhyana* become possible. Do the first thing first, and then the next thing will come by itself."

The holy scriptures recommend that the individual should concentrate on the temple of heart in meditation. Because when *Mantra* calls for the friendship of God, it revolves around the shrine of the Supreme located at the temple of heart. As Lord Kṛṣṇa Himself tells in *Bhagawad Geetā,* chapter 15 (15): "*sarvasya ca 'ham hrdi samnivisto, mattah smritir jnanam apohanam ca*" which means 'I am seated in the hearts of all. I am the source of memory, knowledge and ratiocinative faculty'. Although the Supreme consciousness is the essence of life and resides in each and every little molecule of the body it can be perceived, contacted and experienced only at the heart. The realization of the Supreme Lord at the shrine of the heart is easy and most rewarding experience of life.

It is easy because the individual is not seeking something distant, not something foreign and alien; it is very much known, familiar and one's own Indwelling-Self. The contemplation at the heart has been highly recommended in almost all the spiritual traditions of the world. It is indeed in the subtle realms of consciousness at the *Anāhat cakra* where the aspirant can perceive and experience the presence of the spirit within. When an ardent devotee concentrates at the heart and makes effort to grasp the sound waves of the eternal *nāda* (AUM); he goes into yogic unity with the Indwelling-Soul.

The heart is considered to be the focal point in meditation. Though difficult to perceive, but hidden in the depth of the heart according to Kaṭhopaniṣad is the *atman*. The *atman* which is the only controller is the inner self of all. There are several other hymns in the *Vedas*, which describe the temple of the heart as the shrine in the form of lotus and the innermost cave of the heart. It is strongly believed in almost all religious traditions that it is at the heart where the man is remade. It is by meditating at the heart that the individual is awakened to the Divinity within. When the person is awakened, the Supreme power radiates from him in the form of charismatic warmth, love and compassion. Such an individual becomes very sensitive to the needs of other people and the purity of Divine love emanates from his personality. The other people feel drawn to his awakened shrine and he becomes a channel of sharing divine love with others. The *Upaniṣads* have talked about *hṛidyantar jyoti*. This phrase means that the Lord is experienced as light at the heart. This light represents the Divine Self, radiant and magnificent. The light of life can be actually visualized and experienced only at the heart. This is indeed a very powerful psychic station for integrating psychic energy. The experience of connectedness at the heart centre is considered to be the most valuable accomplishment in the spiritual journey. At the beginning of the meditation session one starts the practice by concentration on the sound of *Aum* or any other *Mantra*. The aspirant is suggested to concentrate at the *hṛdaya akaṣa*—the space between the two breasts. In meditation the individual perceives from within that the beat of his heart and the sound of

Aum have started merging into one another. Gradually the mind also joins the sound and the individual feels settled in the cave of the heart.

A meditation session is a continuation of constant *Mantra Jāp. Mantra Jāp* is preliminary training which is mandatory for going into meditation. In my opinion, there can be nothing such as real meditation unless the individual prepares himself first through constant practice of quiet *Mantra Jāp.*

"Harame dila me makin thā, mujhe mālūma na thā; rage jāṅ se bhī kariṅ thā, mujhe mālūma na thā; maiṅ kahiṅ hūṅ, wo kahiṅ hai, aisā gumāna thā mujhko, maiṅ jahāṅ thā wo wahīṅ thā, mujhe mālūm na thā; dila se pardā jo uṭhā, ho gai rouśana āṅkheṅ, is dila meiṅ hī pardā naśīṅa thā, mujhe mālūm na thā"

''हरमें दिल में मकीं था, मुझे मालूम न था; रगे जां से भी करीं था, मुझे मालूम न था; मैं कहीं हूँ वो कहीं है, ऐसा गुमां था मुझको, मैं जहाँ था वो वहीं था, मुझे मालूम न था; दिल से पर्दा जो उठा, हो गई रौशन आँखें, इस दिल में ही पर्दा नशीं था, मुझे मालूम न था।''

Mantra is the most methodical application. It is indeed the most efficient vehicle that can take us to our goal in meditation. *Mantra* creates a new thought pattern and the mind slowly learns to settle there. Slowly but definitely it peers into the layers of the subconscious and mixes with the knowledge of the Self *(Parā-vidyā)* and enlightens the entire thinking faculty. As the moth after seeing the light never returns to darkness, similarly once the mind is enlightened, it does not involve in ignorance. It likes to rest into the quietness of the Indwelling-Self. *Mantra Jāp* strengthens the individual's unity with the Supreme Self.

When we start the meditation session by repeating *Mantra,* slowly with a gentle breath in and out, we observe our thoughts passing by and leaving many trails behind. At the first stage, we watch our thoughts, then we begin to watch ourselves repeating the *Mantra.* Slowly our mind settles and our breathing also becomes slow, we feel that instead of us repeating the *Mantra* we are only listening to the *Mantra.* At another stage, as we move towards the deeper layers of consciousness, the syllables of our *Mantra* start merging into one another and slowly start disappearing, leaving behind total silence. *Mantra Jāp* if performed systematically, properly, regularly, devotedly, earnestly and lovingly, brings about a sustained single-pointedness more efficiently than all other hasty methods of meditation. A Jāp-conditioned mind rises quickly to the unsurpassable heights of super consciousness in an amazingly short time.

"Moreover, something is or seems,
That touches me with mystic gleams,
Like glimpses of forgotten dreams—
Of something felt, of something here;
Of something done, I know not where;
Such as no language may declare."

—Tennyson

Mantra Initiation

Initiation literally means a beginning. It is an introduction to a spiritual and enlightened way of life. *Mantra* initiation is the guiding light which leads one to self-realization and God-realization. It is a process of awakening and gaining spiritual knowledge through *Mantra*.

Since Vedic times the holy sages in India have emphasized the necessity of a spiritual teacher. They believed strongly that a deep transformation begins in the mind of a disciple at the time of *Mantra* initiation.

In the words of Swami Sivananda, "Although an aspirant may feel nothing miraculous at the time of his initiation, the effect of the *Mantra* given by an enlightened Guru is unfailing. The spiritual guidance that comes with *Mantra* to the aspirant in due time transmutes the individual and the spiritual awakening follows." *Śruti Bhagawati* also supports the same concept.

"Parikshaya lokaan karma chitan, bhahmano nirved maya nasyah kritah kriten, tad vigyanartham

sa gurumeva, bhigachhat samita pani, shrotrayam brahma bishtam". This means that God-realization and self-realization is possible only with the help of an illuminated teacher, through the process of *Mantra* initiation.

Māndukya Upaniṣad describes the same concept in these words: "When taught by a teacher who has realized himself as one with Brahman, a person attains the goal and gets freedom from birth, death and rebirth." Spiritual guidance is indeed the key to self-enlightenment.

As a matter of fact, there is nothing secretive about *Mantras*. Our scriptures, as I stated earlier are full of *Mantras*. This is the reason why some people think that Why not to read a book and select a *Mantra* of our own choice?" Certainly we can do that. Though the use of a self-selected *Mantra* does help the individual but when a *Mantra* is given by a self-realized teacher, it becomes a living seed. For the initiating power of *Mantra* lies in the spiritual *grace* which accompanies the *Mantra* at the time of initiation. That is what makes it special and powerful. The teacher, by his spiritual power, gives life to the word, and thus awakens the spiritual powers in the disciple. That is the secret of the teacher's initiation. Besides, the *Mantra* given by a revered Guru is a *Jāgrat Mantra.* It has been recited by the Guru himself for many years, over a million times; and also it comes from a lineage. As Christopher Isherwood describes, "it's a link in a spiritual chain, for even as the disciple is being initiated by his Guru, so the Guru himself was once initiated by his Guru, and so on backwards, perhaps some holy man of the past whose power is thus being transmitted to the disciple." Another important fact is that the awakening impulse that comes from the words of a teacher cannot be received from a self chosen *Mantra.* The embodied-soul receives enlightenment and awakening only from the words of another pure and contemplative soul. We may study all our lives and select different *Mantra*s according to our taste and temperament, but it can help the individual only to some extent. In the words of Swami Yateshwarananda, "when a spiritually advanced soul repeats the *Mantra*, it becomes charged with its power and it becomes "living". When he gives the *Mantra* to a disciple, the power is transmitted also." He also emphasizes that there are principles to be learned in every activity of life, just as an apprentice needs training in the profession. This is all the more true of spiritual life.

In order to make any type of spiritual progress, one has to go through these four stages of 'Grace'. 1) *Atmā Kṛpā* (Grace of the self), this means personal efforts. 2) *Guru Kṛpā* (The grace of a Guru). 3) *Śāstra Kṛpā* (the understanding of the Śāstras, the holy books and scriptures). 4) *Prabhu Kṛpā* (the grace of the Supreme Divinity). It is indeed a fact that even the understanding of the holy books and the understanding of the Self becomes possible with the grace of a spiritual teacher and the indwelling Divinity.

I have always enjoyed reading this example of relation between the spiritual teacher and the disciple as described by Śrī Rāmakṛṣṇa. He used to say, "As the fabled pearl-oyster leaves its bed at the bottom of the sea and comes up to the surface to catch rain water when the star Swati is in the ascendant. It floats about on the surface of the sea with its shell wide open until it succeeds in catching a drop of the marvellous Swati rain. Then it dives down to the sea-bed and there rests until it has succeeded in fashioning a beautiful pearl out of that raindrop. Similarly, there are some true and eager aspirants who travel from place to place in search of the *Mantra*, the saving word, from a Godly and perfect preceptor (Sadguru) which can open for them the gate of eternal bliss; and in his diligent search, if a man is fortunate enough to meet such a Guru and get from him the much-longed-for *Mantra* that has the power to break all fetters, he leaves society at once and retires into the deep recesses of his own heart and strives there till he has succeeded in gaining eternal peace."

So it's not only the knowledge gathered and absorbed from the books which brings awakening in the life but also the wisdom that comes from the words of the other enlightened soul. The words of the saints do purify us. According to Dr. Radhakrishnan, "Every saint embodies a little of the light of the Supreme and when that light spreads over his whole nature and makes of him an eternal flame, a transparent spirit, then you find that saint becomes a symbol of the Absolute Divine."

As we read in our scriptures that each one of us is made up of gross, subtle and causal body. For example, all of us are very well aware about the omniscience of the indwelling Lord, but seldom make any effort to contact it. For most of us it just exist, but for saints, it is a reality. A God-realized-soul lives at all the three levels of consciousness simultaneously. Since he has contacted the Indwelling-Self he lives in its full awareness. A saint perceives God in everybody and in everything. We find in the life story of Śrī Rāmakṛṣṇa that when Swami Vivekananda, for the first time met Śrī Rāmakṛṣṇa he asked the question: "Have you seen God?" The answer came "Yes, I have seen God". He further added, "even now I see God as clearly as I see you." Only the saint who lives in the consciousness of Divine, has the ability to lead others to the Divine consciousness. Since a saint himself is fully awake, he knows how to awaken other people. Since a saint works in copartnership with God, his attitude is very pure, clean and impartial. *"Sarva bhūta hite ratā".* They see one God standing equal in the entire mankind. They never make any personal judgement about anybody. The saints accept their devotees from all castes, creeds and nationalities. A saint always speaks from the purity of his heart, from the purity of the indwelling Divinity. Carl G. Jung has called this attitude "unprejudiced objectivity." He believed that it is only with an attitude of *"unprejudiced objectivity"* a doctor or a teacher can actually help the other person. It is at this level when you can actually touch the other person and convince him to bring some changes for the better. He writes in his book *Modern Man in Search of a Soul*: "we can get in touch with another person only by an attitude of unprejudiced objectivity. This may sound like a scientific precept and may be confused with a purely intellectual and detached attitude of mind. A truly religious person has this attitude. He knows that God has brought all sorts of strange and inconceivable things to pass, and seeks in the most curious ways to enter a man's heart. He therefore senses in everything the unseen presence of the Divine will. This is what is meant by "unprejudiced objectivity."

Although sometime it happens by chance that we come across a perfect soul and the transformation takes place in us without our being aware of it. This is also due to the subtle influence of the holy sages, but that is indeed very rare. Besides, there are some special individuals who are born initiated. Their spiritual *sanskaras* from their previous births are very strong. Knowingly or unknowingly they are always soaked in the nature of the Divine and do not need any initiation from a teacher. For example, the great devotee Prahlada, Dhruva, Kabir and Meera were definitely born enlightened.

It is important to find a spiritual teacher and receive

the *Mantra* initiation but if a person finds it difficult to seek the grace and guidance of a teacher he can select any appropriate *Mantra.* When the chosen *Mantra* is recited with faith, deep humility and devotion it becomes *jāgrat* and gives very beneficial results in due course of time. The devoted recitation transports the aspirant into transcendental unity and integrates the dormant spiritual energy. It is the sincere practice which brings perfection in *Mantra siddhi*. There are some highly recommended *Mantra*s for initiation and recitation :

ॐ भगवते वासुदेवाय नमः।

Aum Bhagavate Vāsudevāya Namaḥ

ॐ नारायणाय नमः।

Aum Nārāyaṇāya Namaḥ

ॐ श्री रामाय नमः।

Aum Śrī Rāmāya Namaḥ

ॐ महेश्वराय नमः।

Aum Maheśvarāya Namaḥ

ॐ विश्वाय नमः।

Aum Viśvāya Namaḥ

ॐ अचिन्त्याय नमः।

Aum Achintyāya Namaḥ

ॐ श्री ओंकाराय नमो नमः।

Aum Oṁkārāya Namo Namaḥ

ॐ विष्णुवल्लभाय नमः ।

Aum Viṣṇuvallabhāya Namaḥ

ॐ श्रीप्रदाय नमः ।

Aum Śrīpradāya Namaḥ

ॐ भवाय नमः ।

Aum Bhavāya Namaḥ

ॐ श्री परमात्मने नमः ।

Aum Śrī Parmātmane Namaḥ

ॐ त्रिलोकेशाय नमः ।

Aum Trilokeśāya Namaḥ

ॐ वरप्रदाय नमः ।

Aum Varapradāya Namaḥ

ॐ भर्गाय नमः ।

Aum Bhargāya Namaḥ

ॐ श्री वासुदेवाये नमः ।

Aum Śrī Vāsudevāya Namaḥ

ॐ गुणातीताय नमः ।

Auṁ Guṇātītāya Namaḥ

ॐ कृपानिधये नमः ।

Aum Kṛpānidhaye Namaḥ

ॐ मोक्षप्रदाय नमः ।

Aum Mokṣapradāya Namaḥ

ॐ शिवाय नमः ।

Aum Śivāya Namaḥ

ॐ सर्वानन्दाय नमः।

Aum Sarvānandāya Namaḥ

ॐ सच्चिदानन्दाय नमः।

Aum Sacchidānandāya Namaḥ

ॐ दयानिधये नमः।

Aum Dayānidhaye Namaḥ

ॐ श्री केशवाय नमः।

Aum Śrī Keśvāya Namaḥ

ॐ श्री पीताम्बराय नमः।

Aum Śrī Pitāṁbarāya Namaḥ

ॐ निर्मलाय नमः।

Aum Nirmalāya Namaḥ

ॐ ओंकाराय नमः।

Aum Oṁkārāya Namaḥ

ॐ अवनीश्वराय नमः।

Aum Avanīśvarāya Namaḥ

ॐ हरिहराय नमः।

Aum Hari Harāya Namaḥ

ॐ महादेवाय नमः।

Aum Mahādevāya Namaḥ

ॐ परमात्मने नमः।

Aum Parmātmane Namaḥ

ॐ यज्ञमयाय नमः।

Aum Yajñamayāya Namaḥ

ॐ गोपालगोविन्दाय नमः।

Aum Gopālagovindāya Namaḥ

ॐ मंगलमूलाय नमः।

Aum Maṅgalamūlāya Namaḥ

ॐ सदाशिवाय नमः।

Aum Sadāśivāya Namaḥ

ॐ विश्वेश्वराय नमः।

Aum Viśveśvarāya Namaḥ

ॐ श्रीमहागणपतये नमः।

Aum Śrīmahāgaṇapataye Namaḥ

ॐ गणनाथाय नमः।

Aum Gaṇanāthāya Namaḥ

ॐ प्रजापतये नमः।

Aum Prajāpataye Namaḥ

ॐ सत्यसंकल्पाय नमः।

Aum Satyasaṅkalpāya Namaḥ

ॐ बालमुकुन्दाय नमः।

Aum Bālamukundāya Namaḥ

ॐ अनन्तगुणाय नमः।

Aum Anantaguṇāya Namaḥ

ॐ अहिर्बुध्न्याय नमः।

Aum Ahirbudhnyāya Namaḥ

ॐ अनन्ताय नमः।

Aum Anantāya Namaḥ

ॐ श्रीमहालक्ष्म्यै नमः।

Aum Śrīmahālakṣmai Namaḥ.

ॐ सात्त्विकाय नमः।

Aum Sāttvikāya Namaḥ

ॐ ज्योतिरूपाय नमः।

Aum Jyotirūpāya Namaḥ

ॐ शाश्वताय नमः।

Aum Śāśvatāya Namaḥ

ॐ सरस्वत्यै नमः।

Aum Saraswatyai Namaḥ

ॐ निरञ्जनाय नमः।

Aum Nirañjanāya Namah

ॐ भगवते नमः।

Aum Bhagawate Namaḥ

ॐ श्रीकृष्णः शरणं मम।

Aum Śrīkṛṣṇaḥ Śaraṇam Mama

ॐ भुभूर्व स्वः, तत् सवितुर्वरेण्यं भर्गो देवस्य धीमहि, धियो यो नः प्रचोदयात्॥

Aum bhur bhuvaḥ swaḥ, tat savitur vareṇyaṁ bhargo devasya dhīmahi, dhiyo yo naḥ pracodayāt.

Repetition and devoted recitation of any of these *Mantras* surely secures for the devotee the grace of the indwelling Supreme Self. Any one of these *Mantras* becomes powerful and reveals the hidden treasures to any one who repeats with faith, sincere devotion and dedication. *Mantra Siddhi* is attained by repeated practice and with total surrender to the indwelling Supreme Lord.

In the words of Swami Vishnudeva Nanda, "*Mantras* are Sanskrit-invocations of the Supreme Being. Reinforced and propelled by *Jāpa* meditation, they pass from the verbal level through the mental and telepathic states, and on to pure thought energy." Every true *Mantra* fulfils six conditions.

1. It was originally revealed to a sage who achieved Self-Realization through it and passed it down to others. 2. It has a presiding deity and 3. A specific meter. 4. It possesses a *bīja,* or seed, investing it with special power that is the essence of the *Mantra.* 5. It also has dynamic divine power, or Shakti. 6. Lastly, there is a plug that conceals the pure consciousness hidden in the *Mantra.* As soon as the plug is removed by constant, prolonged repetition, pure consciousness is revealed, and the devotee receives the vision of his deity.

Wouldst Thou dwell in this house of mine,
O Thou King of the great Universe?
If this be Thy pleasure,
I shall keep it clean,
Untouched and apart.

—Swami Parmananda

"Avoid what is evil;
Do what is good;
Purify the mind—
This is the teaching
Of the awakened one"

—Suttapitaka Dhammapada

Mantra for Self-purification

What holy *Rāmāyaṇa* states with the help of: "*Nirmal mana jana soi mohe pāvā, mohe kapaṭa chal-chidra na bhāvā*" (निर्मल मन जन सोई मोहे पावा, मोहे कपट छल-छिद्र न भावा), the same Christ states with the help of "*Blessed are the pure in heart for they shall see God.*" A pure heart is indeed a mirror in which we can see reflection of the Supreme-Self. All the spiritual disciplines focus on the purification of the heart. The moment our heart is clean, we do feel God working through us, and others can also feel it. *Nārad Bhakti Sūtra* describes, "*Tirthi kurvanti tirthāni, sukarmi kurvanti karvāni.*" People with a pure heart are indeed the manifestations of God. They impart purity even to the places of pilgrimage. Whatever work they perform, their work reflects purity and spirituality.

In the words of Roy Eugene Davis, "All our efforts to meditate, study, practice self-discipline, etc. are only for the purpose of clearing the mind, so that the light of the soul can be clearly perceived." People usually ask the question, namely, what is a mind? Mind for me is a vessel of thoughts. So when we talk about self-purification, we mean purification of of thoughts. Every individual is known by his thoughts which may be, good or bad compassionate or selfish, considerate or ruthless etc. Good qualities such as love, kindness, sympathy, forgiveness, sweetness of speech originate from good thoughts. These qualities reflect the nature of the Divine and correspond to our innate nature which is pure and uncontaminated. Each one of us likes these qualities, because at the subtle level of our consciousness that's what we are. Clean and pure in all respects. It is the purity of thoughts that brings people together in their original bond—the essence of life. The true nature unites people, brings them closer and makes them caring, sharing and loving. The contaminated and conditioned nature disintegrates people and make them mean selfish, jealous and ruthless. This is what one means by, "*Blessed are the pure in heart for they shall see God.*"

We live in the world circumscribed at each step by commerce, gains, losses, pleasures and pains, whenever we try to make our thoughts pure and clean with moral observances, austerities and *sādhanās,* our thinking faculty becomes receptive to the voice of the Self. We can discover within ourselves the various levels of consciousness leading to the knowledge of the Supreme-Self. It is the experiential knowledge of the Self that makes the God reflected through us. It is the knowledge of the Self that makes the God shine through our speech and action. It is the knowledge of the Self that puts us in harmony with others, with nature and with our own indwelling-Self. It is this knowledge that integrates our entire personality and helps us to work miraculously in all respects.

As we read in our scriptures, Kaundinya's doctrine strongly believed in the *Mantra*'s effect for self-purification, "*Tulyaphalasādhanatvam.*" Although the pure dietary habits, moral observance, charitable deeds, austerities, *yajñas* and other ceremonial worships, play a significant role in process of self-purification, but none of these can give the full benefit unless combined with the constant repetition of the holy *Mantra.* They do purify us to certain extent at the conscious level but hardly clean any of the impurities at the subconscious levels of mind. The thought pattern at the deeper levels are the *saṅskāras* which strongly influence our activities. It is the constant *Mantra Jāp* that makes changes at the different layers of our mind. *Mantra Jāp* accelerates our day-to-day emotions and makes us receptive to the voice of the inner-Self.

Speaking truth is an austerity and it purifies our thoughts. There is a *Mantra* in *Vedas* which has been stated thus: "*Om adbhirgātrāṇi sudhyanti manāsatyen sudhyate*" This Mantra means that we are required to take bath or shower with soap and water for the cleanliness of the physical body; similarly for the purification of mind one must learn to remain firm on speaking truth. Truth purifies our thoughts, because it keeps us connected with the supreme truth, i.e. the God in us. Speaking truth is indeed a great principle of life. Truth is the most honourable virtue. As the truth alone prevails and triumphs, so it is said that '*Satyamev jayate*'. It is this virtue which helps one to develop many more virtuous habits in life. Yudhisthira has been known as Dharamputra, because of his truthfulness. Speaking truth brings fearlessness and security. It gives a lot of self-respect and self-confidence. The sage Gautama accepted Satyakama Jabali as his disciple simply because of his truthfulness. This story is not unknown to us. Satyakama Jabali was an earnest student, when he was asked by the sage Gautama about his parentage and *Gotra,* he confessed and told his teacher that his mother had many men in her life. So he was not aware of his parentage. Sage Gautama was so impressed by the truthfulness of Satyakama Jabali that he accepted him as his disciple.

When we speak truth we in fact reflect the nature of Divine. It uplifts us in our own eyes. It keeps our thoughts pure and uncontaminated. Gandhiji, a great worshipper of truth, writes: "Speaking truth leads one to more awareness—and awareness leads one to Bliss. God combines all the three—*"Sat-cit-ānanda"* (सत् चित आनन्द)—*truth, awareness and bliss.*" Staying firm on truth is very difficult, but one can accomplish this most challenging *sādhanā* (austerity) with the blessings of a spiritual teacher and with the help of regular *Mantra Jāp*.

Regular recitation of *Mantra Jāp* trains the individual to live in God consciousness and awareness. This gives him the strength to speak truth. We observe in our own behaviour that we lie because we don't have the strength of accepting and presenting ourselves the way we are. In order to impress others we constantly lie and pollute our own thoughts. So we harm ourselves more than anybody else. We degrade ourselves in our own estimation. One lie leads to another and thus slowly the individual forms the habit of telling lies. One who lies all the time lives under the impression that others are also lying, such an individual loses faith in other people and does not trust others. Anybody who doesn't trust others is also not trusted. People who frequently speak lie lose faith in themselves. Unknowingly they cheat themselves and harm themselves more than anybody else. Words of Emerson are worthy to quote: "Men suffer all their life under the foolish superstition, that they can be cheated. But it is as impossible for a man to be cheated by any body else but himself."

So we see that it is indeed the habit of speaking truth and living in truth which purifies our thoughts and purifies our mind. It bestows self-purification. Speaking truth and taking pride in it is a very noble austerity, though a very tough ethical discipline. It can be accomplished with the help of *Mantra Jāp*. It's a slow process but it definitely takes shape in due time. The constant humming of *Mantra Jāp* keeps our mind alert and awake. It provides us strength and security and trains the mind to live in spiritual enlightenment. This is my own personal experience and it can be your's too. I like these words from the Bible, "Nothing gives me greater joy than to hear that my children live in the

Truth."

For self-purification, the importance of right food has been highly emphasized in our scriptures. The food we eat does influence not only our physical body but also our subtle body, which is a storehouse of thoughts. Food is called *'anna'* in Sanskrit. *Anna* is related to *prāṇa*—the vital energy. *Prāṇa* energizes the body and is also closely connected with *mana* which is a vessel of thoughts. Our *Śāstras* describe, "*Jaisa khave anna, vaisa hove mana.*" (जैसा खावे अन्न, वैसा होवे मन) The quality of our thoughts is indeed related to the quality of food that we eat. Purity of food does help the purity of thoughts. *Taittiriya Upaniṣad* states the same concept in these words: *Annaṁ na nindyan tat vratam prāṇo vā annaṁ śarirmnnadam prāṇe śarīraṁ pritsṭhataṁ śarīre prāṇaḥ pratiṣṭhitaḥ*. This means that we should always respect the food we eat. *Prana* depends upon food which is eaten by the body. The body rests on *Prana,* and *Prana* rests in the body.

The physical body is called "*Annamaya Koṣa*" which means the sheath that is sustained by food. Śrī Kṛṣṇa declares in the *Geetā* that the food which promotes longevity, purity, strength, health, happiness and good appetite is savoury, oleaginous, substantial, agreeable and liked by *sāttvika* people. Milk and milk products, vegetables, fruits, wheat, barley, grams, rice, almonds, cashewnuts, dates and raisins etc., come under the category of *sāttvika* (pure) food. This group of food produces cheerfulness, purity and emotional clarity which promotes good health in all respects. It energizes the body and keeps the digestive system in perfect order. Such type of food is highly conducive for intellectual clarity, purity and stability of mind.

Foods which are bitter, sour, saline, pungent and dry are liked by people of *rājasika* (passionate) temperament. These types of food do cause sickness and discomfort in the body and mind. The food which is half-cooked or half-ripe, insipid, putrid and polluted is liked by the deluded people of *tāmasika* temperament. This also includes non-vegetarian foods such as meat, fish, eggs etc. These foods have been considered totally unfit for human beings. Human teeth are meant for eating only vegetarian food. The human intestine which is long and narrow is not designed to digest any type of meat. The undigested meat stinks in the stomach and causes many type of diseases. An ignorant person does not care about the adverse effects of food which he eats; for him the taste of palate is the first and foremost priority. He does not mind eating the remnants of food and also sharing his dish with others. For example, some people sit together and eat from the same dish or plate and drink juice or water from the same glass. Such habits do promote infections and are not pure. The *śāstras* describe that the food which has been partly eaten by someone becomes unfit to be taken by another. The *tāmasika* (ignorant) man is usually careless about the quality and quantity of food he consumes.

The type of food consumed by the individual produces positive and negative effects on the body. It influences the physical as well as the subtle body, which is a reservoir of thoughts. The *Chāndogyopaniṣad* describes that the food which is consumed by the individual is assimilated in a threefold process. The coarsest portion becomes the faeces; the middle portion becomes the flesh, and the subtlest portion becomes the mind. So it is advisable that one should eat only that food which can promote the purity of thoughts. Besides, it is not just the ingredient of food which influences the state of mind, but also the procedure in which the food is cooked and consumed. This is one of the reasons why most of the saints and sages prefer to cook their own meal. For example, when a certain recipe is given to five cooks, they exhibit five different results, because each one of them adds his individual thoughts and feelings in the cooked stuff. Good and positive thoughts do produce pleasant and enjoyable taste, and also affect the temperament and health of the person who eats.

Another important factor which influences the mind is the attitude with which the food is consumed. It is very important for a person to hold good and positive thoughts about food, both while cooking and eating. Almost all sacred books of the world recommend many different kinds of hymns, which should be recited, while cooking and also before eating the meal. For example, a prayer of gratitude before eating has been prescribed in almost all the religions of the world, such as, *Thank you God for the world so sweet, Thank you God for the food we eat.* The prayer is a gesture of appreciation and humility towards the benefactor. A simple prayer before eating creates the atmosphere of devotion, love and relaxation for the individual which helps his body in the proper assimilation of food. The holy *Vedas* have also recommended to recite this hymn before eating *Om annapate annasya, dehan mevaisye shushmana prapradataram nodehi de chatush pade*—may the food I eat be beneficial for the body in all respect. The holy sages have emphasized that the individual should recite verse fourteen from chapter fifteen of *Bhagawad Geetā* after he finishes the meal. This verse is recited by placing the middle finger on the naval. *Aham vaisvānaro bhūtva prāṇinam dehaṁ asrītah prāṇapansamayukta pacamy annam caturvidham*. This means that having become the fire *Vaisvanara*, I dwell in the bodies of the living beings, and united with *prāṇa* and *apāna* (the inhalation and exhalation), I digest the four kinds of food. The recitation of this verse helps one in digestion and assimilation of the food.

It is the voice from inside that tells, "treat others as you would like to be treated yourself." It is the voice from inside that tells you to forgive others, that nobody deserves to be treated harshly. As *Mantra* takes hold of our thought process, gradually we become loving, caring and forgiving. It happens effortlessly. We don't have to resort to fighting against our bad habits. They just disappear. The contaminated and confused mind becomes purified and blissful and sings the melody of the inner *nāda* (sound). When an individual keeps his mind busy in recitation of the holy syllables, and, keeps his identity firm with the Supreme, he accelerates his day-to-day emotions. The traps can't pollute his *antahkaraṇa* (thinking faculty). When the previous thick dirt is washed off, it is very easy then to maintain cleanliness in future.

There are so many stories in our history illustrating this truth. The robber named Ratnākara, for example, lived in a jungle terrifying the people around for many miles. People living in the neighbourhood didn't dare to cross the forest in which he lived. His hiding place was under a tree. One day a sage was passing by. As he approached the robber the latter was totally amazed and surprised. After a short heart to heart, conversation, the sage suggested to the robber to recite the "*Rām nām Mantra*." He did not ask the robber to give up whatever he was doing. He only initiated the new disciple into his *Mantra* and left. It was after a few months the sage came back to that forest. While he was passing by, he stopped under the same tree where he had given *Mantra* to his disciple. To his utter surprise, he saw his disciple completely absorbed in meditation. The sage touched the forehead of his disciple. He blessed him and gave him the name Vālmiki. The *Mantra Jāp* washed all the impurities of Ratnākara and the fierce robber became the sage Vālmiki who later wrote the great epic *Rāmāyaṇa*.

Mantra Jāp can purify and clean our heart of all the material contamination, and, can bring us face to face with the Supreme Lord. Literate or illiterate, ignorant or enlightened, rich or poor, men or woman, all can use it with equal benefit. Sometimes it happens that the intellectuals, the so-called learned, well-read individuals fail to accept the spiritual powers of something so simple. It may sound odd to many but it is true that purity of heart, the on-going process of self-purification dawns simply and quickly on people who approach God with total surrender, and do not involve themselves in reasoning. As Paul Brunton writes in his book, *The Spiritual Crisis in Man,* "the human ego must make the first faint beginning to renounce its sovereignty in favour of the Divine overself." He further writes, "after all how can there be peace for anyone if his lower nature still enslaves him, still disturbs his relations with others or disrupts his relation with his own Divine Self."

If people, living in modern sustainable societies, can convince themselves about the utility and power of *Mantra Jāp*, they will come closer to each other. People will become pure, gentler and more forbearing. Purity of heart, will improve the relations between friends and relatives and our world will be a happier and comfortable place. Often people say that first one should become vegetarian and should stop drinking and then start one's spiritual journey. It suggests that first one must learn some ethics and then alone one should start one's spiritual pursuit. I believe the other way. First one should start the *Mantra* recitation and when the name of the Lord starts touching the subconscious level the thought pattern changes and all other changes for ethical discipline start penetrating into our life style one by one. We don't have to wrestle with our bad habits. With the help of *Mantra Jāp* our bad habits start disappearing and self-purification starts manifesting. Similarly the code of ethics for self-purification does not prescribe just going to the temple, mosque or church, it is not just saying loud prayers but it is identifying ourselves with the Supreme-Self. It is living a life which is tuned to the voice of the indwelling-Self. *Mantra Jāp* helps us to identify ourselves with God and slowly the self-purification takes place naturally and automatically.

Regular *Mantra Jāp* keeps us in harmony with our pure spiritual nature. At the beginning the aspirant has to develop consciously the habit but subsequently it just becomes a second nature. The recitation of *Jāp* is felt at all times. It keeps us in touch with the inner-Self and checks all kinds of our stray thought. On one hand it acts like a watchman to check, and on the other to purify every emotion, every impulse before it joins the thinking faculty. As Tagore writes, *I shall ever try to drive, all evils away from my heart and keep my love on flower, knowing that thou hast thy seat in the innermost shrine of my heart*. So it should be our endeavour to culture the mind with rhythm of *Mantra* recitation and nurture the mind with the meaning of *Mantra* recitation. *Mantra* recitation shall make our lives pure, gracious and blissful. Recite the holy name while meditating on the Supreme-Self, you will feel the purification in your mind, in your ego and in every cell of your body. As Swami Rāmakṛṣṇa used to say, "Sing with *bhakti* the hallowed name of the Lord, and the mountain of your sins will vanish, just as a mountain of cotton will burn to ashes and disappear if but spark of fire falls on it."

"All the world's a stage
and all the men and
women merely players.
They have their exits
and their entrances.
Each man in his lifetime
plays many roles."

—Shakespeare

Mantra and self-unfoldment

Know thyself—the most favourite words of the Greek philosopher Socrates are written on the temple of the oracle in ancient Greece. Unfolding the self is the most valuable and the most rewarding gift of life. It is a journey from gross to subtle and then to the subtle-most centre of Self. It is difficult to know the world and everything else around without knowing our ownself in all dimensions. J. Krishnamurti observes, "self-knowledge is the beginning of wisdom. In self-knowledge is the whole universe. It embraces all the struggles of humanity." I am led to believe his thesis because our relation to everything and with everybody around us depends upon our relationship with our ownself.

Lack of self-knowledge is indeed the cause of our many day-to-day problems and frustrations. Dr. Deepak Chopra tells in one of his lectures that "No-body wants to live with a stranger, but unfortunately most of us do live our lives like a stranger with our ownselves. Every person wears many masks and has many forms of armour, those keep his reality confine and unknown to himself." To become that whatever we choose to be is very much possible in our life. We have the power to change the roles which we play in our life. All these can be achieved with the help of *Mantra Jāp*. *Mantra Jāp* which strengthens our relationship with the indwelling Self works as a tool to know more about our ownselves. It helps us to know as how to relate to others and also to discover our dramatic course of life. By self exploration we can easily discover the area of agreement as well as disagreement within our own personality.

We can become more aware of the options available to us, and have more conscious control of how we deal with others and how they deal with us. I am saying this because usually we don't even try to understand ourselves any better than the way we feel we are. People often say, "Life has never been fair to anybody." People often utter, "*Nanak dukhiyā saba samsāra*" (नानक दुखिया सब संसार). Without thinking about the next line of this verse, namely, "*Vo sukhiyā jisa nāma ādhāra*" (वो सुखिआ जिस नाम आधार). The first half means that the life is full of pain and misery but the second half means that he who lives in unity with God, and is soaked in the spirit of *Naam Jāp* is happy and peaceful.

Like our friends, relatives and like everybody else we are, most of the time, preoccupied with selfcreated webs. We are so used to live a complex and unhappy life that we have almost forgotten the taste of happy life. We keep ourselves trapped in our self-created webs, and live a life of bondage and pain, until the grace of God touches our heart. Sometimes this awakening happens by chance. For example, a serious illness and some other painful incident in life gives us the opportunity to become introduced to our inner intelligence and helps us to know more about ourselves. The bliss which flows from our links with the inner-Self brings a lot of awakening and the transformation occurs for better and peaceful living.

Dale Carnegie's description of an incident about his friend Lucil Blake elucidates this truth. According to Dale, "he met Lucil years ago when both of them were studying in the Columbia School of Journalism. One morning she collapsed. It was a heart attack and the doctor told her to lie in bed for one year of complete rest. The very thought of being invalid terrorized her. Her friend explained to her the situation, this being an opportunity for her spiritual growth—something which would not have happened in her whole life otherwise. Lying in bed gave her a chance to get acquainted with her inner-self. During that year Lucil read lots of books, and heard a lot of inspirational commentaries over the radio. Although she had heard all this before but now it reached down inside her with new meanings. She decided to think positively and live by the thoughts of joy, happiness and health. She formed the habit of counting her blessings every morning—something which she had never done before. She valued the gift of life until she feared she was actually going." The positive attitude does begin with self-unfoldment and self-revelation begins by staying in touch with the supreme Self. There is no doubt about it that every time life revitalizes itself and renews itself from our own resources.

The word meditation is becoming very popular these days. Most of the big companies are encouraging their employees to go for aerobics, yoga and meditation sessions. All these activities give the individual a chance to get in touch with his indwelling-Self. For example, Yoga comes from the original word *Yuj* which literally means to commune and to communicate with the inner-Self. The yogic unity in meditation brings a lot of transformation at the various levels of consciousness. It puts the body and mind in tune and helps the individual to be more productive in his work. It improves his relationship with other people and gives him a chance to know more about himself and others.

Understanding God, understanding this universe, understanding others and understanding our own self is one and the same thing. Proper understanding of either of them amounts to understanding of everything. There is a hidden *Brahmānanda* in every *Manuṣya,* a *Nārāyaṇa* in every *nara,* a *Puruṣottama* in every *puruṣa,* a *Devatā* in every *Dānav,* a *Bhagawan* in every *insān, God* in every existence. Dr. Paul Brunton writes, "the only thing asked of every man is to turn about, change the direction of his outlook and face the Overself. Everyone is destined to come into its enlightenment. Once he has found this presence, felt this inspiration and surrender to this power."

At the end of discourse in *Śrīmad Bhagawad Geetā,* Śrī Kṛṣṇa enquires from Arjuna: "O'Partha, have you heard My message with concentrated attention? Has your ignorance been destroyed?" Arjuna answers naturally and spontaneously that his delusion has been dispelled, and he has regained his memory. He feels integrated and is free from all doubts. He tells Srī Kṛṣṇa that he will act according to His instructions. Arjuna's reply indicates his psychological transformation and inner stability. He feels awakened once again to the consciousness of the Divine. Arjuna feels introduced to a higher truth, wherein his memory returns with a new concept of truth and *svadharma.* He perceives that he has regained his lost memory of his perennial connectedness with the Supreme-Soul. He comprehends the essentiality of his nature and re-evaluates the entire situation. The very first word of his answer to Srī Kṛṣṇa is *naṣṭo mohaḥ*—this means that the delusion born out of attachment, ignorance and false identification has been destroyed. The life that seemed like a useless burden, now feels like a great blessing, to be used in the service of the Lord. Arjuna feels very encouraged and enthusiastic about performing his duties.

Arjuna's spontaneous answer in these words *smritir labdha* is very significant. *Smritir* literally means memory and *labdha* means regained. *Smrtirlabdha* means the veil has been removed and the reality is being revealed. Arjuna tells Srī Kṛṣṇa that with His grace, he has regained his memory and realized his true identity. When the individual regains his awareness of the Supreme-Soul, he becomes blessed with the experiential knowledge of his own immortality. His doubts are dispelled and his fears are destroyed. The person moves forward without hesitation, quite intuitively, courageously, spontaneously and harmoniously. There are some beautiful words by a Sufi poet :

Dariyā kī mouja se lahara uthi, aur ulata kara bahāra se kahane lagī, mai tujh se huī āur tujha me phanā, mai aura nahī, tu aur nahi.

दरिया की मौज से लहर उठी, और उलट कर बहर से कहने लगी, मैं तुझसे हुई और तुझमें फना, मैं और नहीं, तू और नहीं।

—The identification of the isolated wave, dissolves at the dawn of realizing itself as an integral part of the river.

This is an experience of *ātmabodha*—the knowledge of the Self. It is being awakened to one's own completeness. It is the experience of being restored to the wholeness in which the individual soul resumes his unity with the Supreme-Soul. Arjuna feels totally oriented to an absolutely new concept of life. His entire outlook is changed for the better. He feels confident and integrated in all respects. He gives up his separate existence and identifies himself with the work of the Lord. A revelation of this magnanimity is indeed the prerogative of each and every individual. This rediscovery of one's own essential nature is possible for everyone, only if the person become introduced to the grace of the Indweller.

The grace of the Supreme Lord lies perpetually within the various sheaths of one's own awareness. It lies veiled beneath one's own individualized, egocentric limitations. In the process of constant *Mantra* recitation with faith and devotion for the indwelling-Self, when the person resorts to the grace of the Lord, the purity and the essentiality of his own divine nature unfolds itself and becomes available to the individual. It is a very personal experience of the indwelling Divinity at the exalted level of inner awakening. It is the communion of the *'nara'* with his eternal companion *'Narayana'*. It is the transcendence of the individual soul into the majesty of the Supreme-Soul. It is the transmutation of the limited identification into the infinite cosmic identification. In moments of self-revelation the embodied-self that has descended earlier into the limitations of mind and body, now wakes up once again to the majesty of its own infinitude.

The sages proclaim the knowledge of the Self to be secretive, because it remains foreign to the individual until a genuine endeavour is made by the aspirant and the acceptance from the Lord becomes possible. Any endeavour which is made with the purity of heart, unveils the knowledge of the self, and the redemptive process of grace becomes active and available to the individual. When the devotee remembers the Lord incessantly, with recitation of his holy *Mantra,* his mind becomes concentrated on the Lord and he starts identifying himself with the Supreme. When the mutual love is strengthened with the indweller, the process of self-realization takes place automatically.

It is indeed a fact that every individual is necessarily incomplete and fragmented until he resorts to the majesty of the Supreme Self. The dissipated endeavours of a disintegrated individual are the expressions of his inner turmoil, leaping in various directions, with repeated search for satisfaction and inner completeness. He moves agitatedly here and there in quest of something not quite clear to his own-self. The performance of his work explains his dissatisfaction, restlessness and inner emptiness. The radical cure for all his problems lies in his conscious re-orientation and re-association with the source of life. The unity with the indwelling-Self helps the individual to comprehend the prime truth in its completeness; it is the blessed experience of the consciousness of the Supreme-Lord by the totality of the being. The faculty of reason deprives the individual from the comprehension of the Infinite, but the loving devotion prepares the individual for a blessed experience of the Divinity by willingness and acceptance. It is the perennial consciousness of the Infinite in thoughts, words and deeds, which makes the realization of Self to be natural and effortless.

The practice of *Mantra Jāp* helps us to know the existence of God and also experience our essential, pure, unconditioned nature. This is how the mind opens itself effortlessly to a new world of awareness. In the words of Roy Eugene Davis, "the purpose of self unfoldment, however, is not to learn to do what others might feel to be extraordinary, but rather to learn to do ordinary things extraordinarily well." With self knowledge and understanding, a doctor becomes a good caring doctor, a teacher becomes a competent sympathetic teacher, and a lawyer becomes a good helpful lawyer.

The *Mantra Jāp* helps us to put together the best available in us and then helps us to use it by keeping in mind global welfare. As *Mantra Jāp* keeps us constantly connected with God and with everyone else around us so global welfare is kept in mind. Our understanding of other people depends upon how much we understand ourselves. Our honesty in dealings, kindness, generosity, compassion towards other people depends on how much we are honest with ourselves. Only clear and honest understanding of our ownselves allows an honest relationship with rest of the universe.

Since *mantra jāp* keeps us linked with our inner Self it provides us a good understanding of our ownself. *Mantra Jāp* brings people together. It joins people by the common bond they share. The little children, for example, are so trusting, honest, forgiving, clean and simple at heart, because most of the times they are exhibiting what they really are. There is no mask of artificiality. There is no mask of being someone else. Since they are in constant touch with God, their spontaneous behaviour is based more upon the pure, essential nature of the indwelling-Self. Their behaviour is always natural, warm, simple, innocent, forgiving and compassionate, simply because they are more closer to their true nature than the adults.

"baccae mana ke sacce, sare jaga ke āṅkha ke tare, yeh vo nanhe phūla hai jo, bhagvāna ko lagte

pyāre, insān jaba taka baccā hai, taba taka samjho saccā hai, jyon jyon uskī umara badhe, taba taba mana para maila cadhe."

"बच्चे मन के सच्चे, सारे जग की आँख के तारे, ये वो नन्हे फूल हैं जो, भगवान को लगते प्यारे, इन्सान जब तक बच्चा है, तब तक समझो सच्चा है, ज्यों-ज्यों उसकी उमर बढ़े, तब तब मन पर मैल चढ़े।"

As we grow older, our identification with body, ego and the outer world becomes so strong that we forget our own identity. Each person wears several masks and plays different roles in life. We often complain why human relations are so complex? But who can be stated as cause of this complexity? No one but ourselves is the cause of this complexity. Just be yourself is the answer. So in order to go back to our real nature, we have to remember that there is a reality underlying our mask, so it is the grasping of that truth, being one with that truth which makes a human being worthwhile. It is the grasping of that truth which connects us back to where we belong; it is the grasping of that truth which unfolds our true nature to us and makes our life worthwhile. In the words of Dr. Radhakrishnan, "the fulfilment of man consists in what *Geetā* calls *Brahma sparsha,* living in the consciousness of the self. It is an extensive feeling, it is a perpetual experience, it is an intuitive communion with the Supreme."

Almost all the prayers of the world talk about the need for self awareness. One saint puts it in the following words: "we are born once from the womb of our mother; we are born a second time from our own self-unfoldment." To some people self-unfoldment occurs during their illness from the desire to be free from physical pain. There are others who are inquisitive for self-knowledge in order to extend their influence upon others. No matter, whatever the reason it transforms our outlook in all respects, and also no matter whatever the method they all correspond to the basic fact that self-unfoldment takes place from our own alignment with the indwelling Supreme-Self.

Mantra Jāp is the spark of positive energy and it can surely enlighten us if we learn to direct its force properly. As Lord Buddha has said, "Learn to light thy lamp." We should always remember that ignorance is darkness, and self-knowledge is light which is peculiarly a human prerogative. It is essentially ours and at our demand, it only needs to be manifested and then it works by itself. Just as the ancient man knew that fire existed in the flint but friction was necessary to bring it out. Exactly like that with the friction of *Mantra Jāp* when the flame of wisdom is lighted self-unfoldment, self-realization and self-enlightenment comes very effortlessly and naturally. This is called Divine-revelation in many religious traditions of the world.

Om, asato mā sad gamay; tamaso mā jyotir gamay; mrutyormā amṛtam gamaye.

ओम, असतो मा सद् गमयः।

तमसो मा ज्योतिर्गमयः।

मृत्योर्मा अमृतम् गमयः।

"O' God, lead me from untruth to truth, From darkness to light and From bondage to immortality."

The Great Gāyatrī Mantra

गायत्री महामन्त्र

ॐ भूर्भुवः स्वः। तत्सवितुर्वरेण्यं भर्गो देवस्य धीमहि।
धियो यो नः प्रचोदयात्॥ —यजुर्वेद ३६.३

Aum bhūrbhuvaḥ swaḥ tatsaviturvareṇyaṁ bhargo devasya dhīmahī dhiyo yo naḥ pracodayāt. —*Yajurveda 36.3*

The glory of *Gāyatrī* has been described throughout the *vedic* literature. Meditation with the chants of *Gāyatrī* connects us to the throbbing Being who is the essence of life.

The recitation of the first three words, namely, *bhūr, bhuvaḥ* and *swaḥ*, connects the individual to all the three levels of consciousness. These three levels are physical, psychological and spiritual. *Bhūr* symbolizes the physical body composed of five elements: earth, water, air, ether and energy. With prayer one asks for complete harmony and support with cosmic forces. The word *bhuvaḥ* stands for thought process as a controller of astral body or the inner nature. *Swa* stands for the indwelling light the Supreme-self. *Gāyatrī Jāp* brings harmony at all the three levels of consciousness. It keeps electrifying thoughts with spiritual power. It purifies thoughts, speech and action.

In *Gāyatrī mantra* the aspirant calls upon the divine mother—*Savitur* for inner enlightenment, clarity of vision, purity of mind and intellect, precision of thoughts, inner integrity and right guidance into the activities of daily life.

"...Na hi Jnanena sadrasm pavitramiha vidyate, tatsvayam yogasamsiddhah kalenatmani vindati..."
(Verily there is no purifier in this world, like knowledge; he who is perfected in yoga realizes it in his Self in due course of time).

"...Sraddhavaml labhate jnanam tatparah samya tendriyah, jnanam labdhva param santim acirena 'dhigacchati..."
(He who has faith and has mastered his senses, devoted to spiritual practices attains knowledge; and having attained knowledge he quickly attains Supreme peace)

—Shrimad Bhagawad Geeta
Chapter 4, Verse 38-39

Significance of understanding the meaning of Mantra

Pātañjali *Yoga Sutra* states: *"Tad Jāpas tad artha bhavanam"* (तद जपस्तदर्थ भावनम्)। These words of Rishi Pātañjali are self-explanatory. It explains that *Mantra Jāp* should be performed by meditating on the meaning of *Mantra*. To concentrate on meaning is very important in *Mantra Jāp*. This is so, because theoretical recognition is one thing and practical assimilation is quite different. So in order to achieve practical assimilation, we must allow the truth to penetrate our understanding. The human nature is a mixed formulation of many aspects—body, mind, intellect, and spirit. These faculties are usually in conflict with one another. In order to bring these faculties together and to let them work in coordination, it is indeed important to understand the meaning of our *Mantra*. As Buddha said: "*Parikṣya bhikṣavo grāhyam mad vāco nātha gauravat*". "Do not accept my words out of regard for me; *pariksya*—accept after proper understanding and contemplation.

Recitation of *Mantra* with the proper understanding

of meaning helps the intellect to be used at the service of the contemplative end. The meaning of *Mantra* helps the intellect to merge into the central core of the mind, and then the mind flows into the transcendental consciousness. As we know, the whole purpose of reciting the sacred word is to free oneself from all the false conditioning; from all limiting layers and be one with the infinite. So when we start reciting the *Mantra* soaked in its meaning, our thoughts move round the meaning of the words and slowly but definitely our thoughts start taking the shape of the words and their meaning. Faithfully and lovingly repeated over and over, it leads us to discover our true nature. It is not a way of just doing something mechanically but being a part of it. It is like being and becoming one with it.

Therefore, *Mantra* must be composed of the right sacred syllables, correctly pronounced (in the mind) by the disciple. As Sir John Woodroffe, a scholar in *Mantra Śāstra* explains, "by constant *Jāp* of *Mantra*, with full meaning in thoughts, the mind is actually shaped into those thoughts and is made pure for the time being." By constant practice the mind becomes full of those specific thoughts to the exclusion of everything else. The energy released from each word of the *Mantra* splits and takes forms and patterns of our choice. Both the *Mantra Jāp* and the experience that it brings with it are important for spiritual growth. It helps one to live in the *Mantra* and take full benefit out of it. Swami Satyasangananda Saraswati describes in his book—*Light on the Guru and Disciple Relationship:* "When a disciple receives a *Mantra* from his guru, he understands it mentally. Then he practises it with his breath and in every part of his being until the *Mantra* overpowers his existence, and gradually the consciousness of the disciple is transformed. The previous consciousness which was dissipated, broken and disintegrated, is consolidated into the form of the *Mantra.*"

Without understanding the full meaning of Mantra, *Mantra Jāp* takes us only upto a certain point. At this point the intellect starts questioning, "what next?" Without proper understanding of the meaning of Mantra, we do not enjoy the essence. *Mantra Jāp* in this situation becomes monotonous and boring. But with meaning emerges the taste of each and every word, and we actually enjoy it. It also satisfies the demand of our intellect as to "why am I doing it, and what am I actually experiencing?" This concept has been described by *Yaska* in his *nirukta*: "*stharunai bharbar kila bhudhitya ved na vijanate yotharm yothraga se, sankalam bhadrmashnute sa nakmeni jyana vidhutepamama*" it means he who repeats the *Mantra* without understanding its meaning is like an ass carrying a load of sandal wood; it knows only the weight of the load, but it does not enjoy the fragrance.

So in order to enjoy our *Mantra* and in order to assimilate it in our understanding, it is very important to understand the meaning of our *Mantra.* In the words of Swami Satprakashananda, "Every word is a form of inner consciousness. The word Love is not just L-O-V-E, a combination of four letters. It is something more than that. The word T-R-E-E is not just something which you see before your eyes or the sound that you hear with your ears, but something deeper. So these words being heard or spoken do awaken the inner consciousness provided you know their meaning. As you understand the true meaning of God or Jesus or Kṛṣṇa or Rāma, the very utterance of any of these will awaken the inner consciousness."

In *Chandogya Upaniṣad* one may find that *Śruti Bhagawati* supports this concept "*...śat lakṣa prajāpatopi tasya mantro na sidhyati...*" Understanding the meaning of Mantra helps us in realizing the essence of it and thus attaining the full benefit. And also ".......*Mantrārth Mantrasya caitenyaṁ yo na jānāti sādhakaḥ sa mokṣaḥ na labhyate*......" Which means that in order to achieve perfection, it is necessary to know and understand the meaning of Mantra.

These statements, however, does not mean that one should be aware of the grammatical meaning of every single syllable to be benefited by it, but it is very important for the words to be intelligible in true sense. In order to achieve the maximum benefit from *Mantra Jāp,* it is definitely important to understand the words which enable us to meditate and satisfy our thinking faculty. For example, we may not understand the meaning of *Gāyatrī* as a sage does, but still some explanation helps in order to get the full benefit of it. As Śrī Kṛṣṇa himself says in the *Bhagawad Geetā,* chapter 12 (12): "...*sreyo hi jnanam abhyasaj jñāna dhyānaṁ visisyate*..." That alone which is performed and recited with understanding, faith and proper insight, becomes spiritually effective.

In the words of Swami Tapasyananda, "Every word is the expression of some idea or desire that arises in us. The *Mantra* stands for the spiritual urges of man, just as an ordinary word when heard or uttered can arouse a certain idea or desire in us. So also the *Mantras* can arouse in us our latent spiritual tendencies." He further writes, "that in order to establish a definite relationship between the sound, symbol and the holy idea, the idea must come forward, the very moment you touch the key of the sound symbol." It is our association with the meaning of *Mantra* that makes the *Mantra Jāp* lively, interesting, beneficial and enjoyable.

There are several types of *Mantras* and all the components of the *Mantra* represent various aspects of the infinite consciousness. For example, the *deity Mantra Jāp* holds that by repeating the syllables with accurate pronunciation in mind, the *Mantra* evokes the presiding deity. The mantra, *Aum namaḥ śivāya* or *Aum namo Nārāyaṇam* would produce the form of *Śiva* or *Viśnu* respectively. *Aum namaḥ śivāya* is a very popular *Mantra* chanted all over India, specially at South India. Another popular *Mantra* among the Buddhist is *Aum mani padme hum.* This Buddhist *Mantra* refers to concentration in the lotus of the heart.

There are *bīja Mantras* which are used to comprehend the nature of different centres of consciousness. *"Bīja"* means "seed" which in turn signifies the spark of energy stored in each *cakra*. As the words of these *bīja Mantras* vibrate in the psychic centres, a new idea is introduced in our thinking process. The latent power at every *cakra* in our body is aroused by a specific *bīja Mantra.* These *cakras* are the psychic centres in our body. The first one is located at the base of the spine known as *Mūladhārā Cakra.* On the disc at this point, there is a triangle which emanates white and golden light. One perceives the luminous white rays going in all directions but specifically pointed upward. This station has the elemental qualities of earth. While meditating at this root centre, one feels charged with the primal energy and also the elemental (symbolic) qualities of earth, which is firmness, steadiness and patience. The energy at this point is perceived and visualized as the deep red lotus with four petals. The Sanskrit letters written on the petals are *sām, śam, vam* and *śam*. The *bīja Mantra* of *Mūladhāra Cakra* is *lam* and in the centre of this lotus is a *Śivaliṅgam*. A golden colour serpent with three and a half coils encircles the *Śivaliṅgam*. Its tail is tucked in the mouth. *Mūladhāra* psychic station is presided by the creator of the universe, the Brahma Himself. The presiding Goddess at this centre is Dākini who controls the element of skin in the body. In meditation with the proper alignment of the spine, the primal energy is aroused from the base and directed to travel upwards through all the other stations along the *śuṣumnā nādi*.

The second psychic station along the *śuṣumnā* is the *swadhisṭhāna Cakra*. *'Swa-dhisṭhāna'* literally means 'one's own abode'. This station is perceived and visualized in meditation as a lotus with six petals around a disc and with the symbol of crescent in the centre. The Sanskrit *bīja Mantras* on these petals are *bam, bham, mam, yam, ram* and *lam*. The *bīja Mantra* of this psychic station is *vam*. The presiding Lord of the centre is Viśṇu and the presiding deity is Rakini who controls the element of blood. The colour is vermillion and it is related with the survival of the race. The elemental quality of *Swadhisṭhāna* is water. This station is connected with the conscious and unconscious thoughts of the present and also with the latencies of the many previous lives. It is possessed with the present and remote memories. It is indeed the storehouse of the most primitive and instinctive behaviour which relates to the survival of the species. This psychic station is related to sexual urge and to the organs of reproduction and excretion. The exact location of this *cakra* is at the level of the pubic bone or we can say coccyx at the distance of about four inches in the front part of the body from *Mūladhāra*.

The third psychic station along the *śuṣumnā* is the *Maṇipūra cakra*. *Maṇipūra* combines two words. *'Maṇi'* literally means the 'jewel' and *'pūra'* means the 'city'. When combined together it means the city of jewels. Fire (heat) is the element for this *cakra* and the colour is bright yellow. The Lord of *Maṇipūra* is *Rudra* and the deity is *Lākini* who controls flesh in body. It is perceived and visualized as the bright, scarlet colour lotus with ten petals. The Sanskrit words written on these petals are *dam, dham, nam, tam, tham, dam, dham, nam, pam* and *pham*. The *bīja Mantra* of this psychic station is *Rāma*. It is situated at the level of the navel in front of the body, corresponding to a centre on the spine. Meditating at this point enables the individual to enhance the elemental qualities of fire such as purity and vitality.

The next one is the *Anāhata Cakra*. *Anāhata* means the unstruck. This is the root spot of all sounds. It is located between the two breasts known as the heart centre. This psychic centre divides the body in Northern and Southern hemispheres. It is at this centre that the person is remade spiritually, emotionally and ethically. It is the focal point of emotional and psychological maturity. It is perceived and visualized by the meditator as a blue lotus with twelve petals. The Sanskrit *bīja Mantras* inscribed on these petals are *kam, kham, gam, gham, nam, cham, chham, jam, jham, nam, tam* and *tham*. The *bīja Mantra* for meditation at this specific centre is *yam*. The Lord of the centre is *Īśa* and the deity is Kākini. It is felt to be located within the spine corresponding to the point located behind the two breast bones. It is perceived and visualized in front of the chest and also inside the spine along the route of *śuṣumnā*. This *cakra* can be noticed as the star of David, shooting forth its rays all around. The air is the element of this psychic station.

The fifth *cakra* is the *Viśuddhi Cakra*. As the term explains, it is the centre of purification. In meditation it is perceived and visualized as a violet lotus with sixteen petals. These are inscribed with the Sanskrit *bīja Mantras* such as *am, am, im, im, um, um, rim, rim, lrim, lrim, em, aim, om, aum, am* and *ah*. The *bīja Mantra* of this *cakra* is *ham*. Śiva and Pārvati combined together preside over the centre and the deity is Sakini. It is located in the region of the throat, along the route of *śuṣumnā*. At this psychic station one experiences drops of nectar dripping from the *Brahamaranda*. Some yogis do taste the nectar very consciously by rolling the tongue backward to the very far end of the throat in Khechri Mudra. When the tip of tongue is turned backward into the throat, it tastes the blissful elixir of life *(amṛtam)* and feels exhilarated, and in some cases also a bit intoxicated. Some meditators who sit in meditation for a long time at stretch, receive their full nutrition from this blissful Divine elixir. The taste of this blissful elixir can't be described in words and also cannot be compared with any other taste in the world. It supersedes all other tastes of the material world. It renders peace and contentment. The nectar emanates from the *Lalana cakra* and drips at the point located in the upper palate, right at the base of the tonsils. Ether is the element of *Viṣuddhi Cakra*.

The sixth psychic station located between the two eyebrows is known as *Ājñā cakra*. It is also known as the command centre. In general it is called the eye of intuition. In the words of Swami Abhedananda, "Intuition is that power by which the subjective mind can perceive the result without reasoning and without questioning". Meditation at this centre enables the individual to observe and experience almost all the events simultaneously, at the physical as well as at spiritual levels of consciousness. This psychic station is experienced and visualized as a silver blue lotus with two petals. The Sanskrit *bīja Mantras* written on these petals are *ham* and *kṣam*.

The *bīja Mantra* of this centre is the holy syllable *'Aum'*. Śiva is the Lord of the centre and the presiding deity is Hākini who controls the subtle mind. At the centre of this *cakra* is visualized blue lotus with white tiny crescent moon. The element for this *cakra* is mind. It is at this point that the psychic currents *idā* and *piṅgalā* are integrated and the breath-flow is regulated to bring the mind under conscious control. The three red lines running from top to bottom indicate the triad of Nature. The holy syllable AUM can be seen in the middle of these lines. This centre connects one with the remote and present memories and also enables the individual to see in future. This is considered to be the most important centre of spontaneous meditation. Concentration at this point helps the person to understand the depth, beauty and the joy of the spiritual unfoldment. Awakening at this centre acquaints the individual with his own inherent potential. Meditation at this point between the eyebrows, known as *bhrumādhya,* awakens the desire for liberation, salvation and *mokṣa.*

The seventh centre along the *śuṣumnā* is known as *Sahaśrarā*. It is the seat of consciousness which holds all the other *cakras* within itself. It is like a radiant dome at the crown of the head. It is at this point the *Vedic* sages used to grow a long tuft of hair. The ancient *Rishis* used to comb the hair upward and role at the top of the head, to protect this special soft spot, where the spiritual energy is stored. Starting from *Mūladhāra* to this seventh *cakra*, *Sahaśrarā* is the psychic passage which can be perceived and visualized during meditation. Only a spark of the dormant energy from the *mūladhāra* can open up this entire passage along the *śuṣumnā*. *Sahaśrarā,* as the name denotes, is a lotus of a thousand petals extending in almost all directions; on these petals, are the Sanskrit alphabets. The element of this *cakra* is pure consciousness and the colour is shining red. A *Śivaliṅgam* can also be visualized in the centre as the seat. A meditator by focusing his attention on the sound can make the *Mantra* flow uninterruptedly and effortlessly. Although the constant repetition of these *Mantras* engages the mind but does not yield lasting benefit.

There are *Mantras* those are known as *mahāvākya* and given by a spiritual teacher to his disciple in initiation. *Mahāvākyas* can be translated in English as great sentences or utterances or combination of some highly sacred words. These *Mantras* can set up very powerful vibrations in the body and verbally assert union with the pure consciousness. The commonly given *mahāvākyas* are "*tat tvam asī*"—that thou art; "*ahaṁ brahamāsmī*"—I am brahman; *Prajñanam brahman*—Brahman is pure consciousness;— "*ayaṁ ātmā brahman*"—my inner self is Brahman; "*sohaṁ*"—I am He or I am That. All these *Mantras* are indeed very popular and used by the holy sages for initiation. In these, the sound flows very easily with the breath which makes it easier to assimilate with the thought.

The *Jāp* of these *Mantras* brings a lot of questions before the mind of the aspirant and sometime even discouragement. For example, if we keep repeating "*tattvamasī*"—that thou art. The questions arise: who is that? Who is he? What is the relationship between the two? Though the great masters have discussed these questions in detail but ordinary people find difficulties in comprehending these concepts. For example, the *Mantra 'aham brahma asmi'*, I am *Brahman,* here which 'I' we are talking about, which 'I' is *Brahman*, the 'I' that says, I started this mission, I am the most learned person, I have followers all around. If I feel I am the doer then I cannot experience at the same time, that I am the *Brahman*.

Lord Kṛṣṇa makes it very clear in Geeta that as long as there exists identification with the body, mind and ego—the experience of the indwelling Supreme Soul is very difficult. In order to experience the holy communion with the indwelling-soul, the feeling of 'I' and 'Mine' has to be replaced with the feeling of 'Thou' and 'Thine'. It is a training of accepting the presence of Lord and also a training of living in the consciousness of God. The bliss of living a life in the consciousness of the Divine is certainly very rewarding, but it does not take place all at once. There is a process. It is a step by step spiritual progress. The individual has to learn to live in the presence of God at each and every moment of his life. Swami Chinmayananda has expressed the same so lucidly,"a dancer never forgets the rhythm of the drum to which she keeps steps, a musician is ever conscious of the background hum. Similarly a devotee is advised not to take up religion as a part-time entertainment or as a temporary escapism, but to consider the Lord as the supreme goal to be achieved in and through life." It is the spontaneous love for the Divine, the spirit of service for the Divine which brings transformation in the attitude of the individual. Alignment with consciousness of the Divine educates the mind to operate directly under the guidance of the Supreme Divinity.

It is indeed very important that the aspirant's approach to *Mantra Jāp* has to be very humble, polite and with total surrender. The approach should combine the spiritual, physical and psychological levels all at the same time. In other words, the body, mind and intellect has to work simultaneously. It is the approach with love and devotion which helps the aspirant to rise above the limitations of the physical body and to live totally absorbed in the subtlest levels of consciousness. As the absorption increases in intensity, the false titles start dropping one by one. As our relationship with the indwelling-Self strengthens, our relationship with the body and its titles becomes weak. In the re-oriented awareness of the supreme-Self with constant *Mantra Jāp* the concept of I and Mine is automatically replaced by Thou and Thine. Our words slowly become our experience, and experience takes charge of the whole being. It is being and becoming. In the words of Tulsidas , "*so jaanat jo tumhi janai jaanat tumhein tumhi ho jaai*" (सो जानत जो तुम्ही जनाई, जानत तुम्हें तुम्ही हो जाई)।

In order to achieve full benefit of *Mantra Jāp,* it has to be right combination of words, sufficiently intelligible and recited with love and devotion. *Mantra Jāp* with full meaning in mind creates vibrations which make the mind joyous and connects it to its source. As Ellison Banks Findly writes, "*Mantra* is true if—and only—it is formulated with the deepest, most profound understanding possible, that is, with insight arising from the heart. And, if it is indeed fashioned from the heart, the theory goes, it will in some way touch upon the riddles of the world in which man lives, giving power over those things that remain mysterious."

There are several other well-known *Mantras* given by the holy saints and sages to their disciples. These *Mantras* always begin with the holy syllable AUM. AUM is uttered in a pitch higher than the rest of the syllables. AUM has been exalted highly in the *Vedas*, the *Upaniṣads*, *Geetā* as well as in other scriptures.

Srī Kṛṣṇa explains in the *Geetā* that *Aum-Tat-Sat* has been declared to be the trifold designation of the Absolute. *Aum-Tat-Sat*—the three words—indicate three aspects of the absolute Divinity. *Aum,* as described earlier, is the holy syllable which represents the transcendental Supreme Self. All the hymns in *Vedas* and in almost all other sacred scriptures always start with the holy syllable AUM. In the words of Eugene Davis, "OM is the highest *Mantra* to contemplate in meditation because by merging in OM we can flow our attention back to the field of God. OM can be heard as the background sound of Nature. It is the sound from which all other sound-frequencies emerge and into which they return. OM meditation can be used by devotees of any religion or philosophical persuasion because it is beyond all contrived names or forms of God and beyond all concepts of God".

It is believed that the holy syllable Aum symbolizes the triad in space and time. "A" stands for *adimata* meaning the beginning, "U" stands for *utkrishta*—the sustenance; and "M" symbolizes the *mitti*—the dissolution. Yet another theory states 'A' to be symbolic of *vāc*—meaning word; 'U' represents *mana*—which means mind, 'M' represents *prāṇa*—the breath. According to *Māndukya Upaniṣad,* 'A' stands for the conscious level of wakefulness; 'U' stands for the dream stage; and 'M' for sleep stage. The scriptures describe that when the person pronounces these letters in harmony, he catches the energy of the half syllable (*ardhabindu)* which leads the individual into silence. The perfect silence is the fourth stage of consciousness known as *Turiya*. This is the state of union and communion with the indwelling Divinity.

According to Joseph Campbell, "concentration on the sound of Aum connects the person to the throbbing being—the power which is omniscient and omnipresent. All the vowels have come out of the sound of AUM and all the consonants are the images and the fragments of the sound". AUM is the primordial *nāda*. All the notes in music have originated from the vibrating *nāda* of AUM-M-M." The sound of AUM has been the primordial sound which was heard in deep meditation by the sages of antiquity. The great mother Gāyatrī has been revealed from the holy syllable AUM and from Gāyatrī has emanated the *Vedas*. The sound energy of the holy syllable AUM connects us with the cosmos, as well as to the deepest mysteries of the Supreme-Self.

In the performance of any penance or ritual and worship, the individual is suggested to begin the worship with the holy syllable AUM; which initiates the spirit of surrender and essential unity. The significance of beginning the hymn with the holy syllable symbolizes the Lord Himself to be the centre of importance in every act of life. According to Swami Chinmyananda, "To cherish in our mind the divine awareness and the absolute supremacy of the infinite, as expressed in AUM, is to add purpose and meaning to all the acts of sacrifice, charity and austerity. To invoke in mind the divine concept of the Absolute is to free the personality from its limited fields of egocentric attachments. When a mind is thus liberated from its limitations, it becomes more efficient in all austerities, more selfless in all *Yajñas,* and more liberal in all charities".

The recitation of AUM liberates the thinking faculty from its superficiality and the mind settles in the dedicated performance of the *yajña* and penance. The attitude of the person becomes pure and honest, and the act of his penance becomes dedicated, and harmonious. In general, the knowers of the *Vedas* and other holy scriptures know the techniques of perceiving a clear and vivid resonance of the sound of AUM in their mind. They always begin the recitation of each and every hymn, with the sacred sound of AUM.

As to the meaning of my personal mantra these are syllables of deep humility very rich in meaning. My personal *Mantra* is: **ओं नमो भगवते वासुदेवाय नमः। Aum Namo Bhagvate Vāsudevāya Namaḥ.**

It will probably take many pages to describe the meaning and essence of this *Mantra*. Each word pays homage to the Supreme Being in which the entire universe is closely linked. AUM, the initial syllable, connects one with the universal spirit—the supreme cosmic reality. *Namo* is total surrender, devoid of ego, which touches the cosmic Self with humble salutations. The other three words prepare and purify the mind for the holy communication and communion with the Supreme-Self. It generates love and devotion towards God and also oneness and compassion toward the whole universe. While reciting my *Mantra* I offer my salutation to the one who resides in the hearts of all. I salute to the Supreme Lord who resides in each and every little molecule of the universe. I feel myself an expanded being. My *Mantra* extends my relationship with the entire universe. I do feel and experience that the syllables of my *Mantra* revolve within and without, inside and outside. Each word transmits its rays in all directions. My heart is overwhelmed with gratitude for the peace, happiness and fulfilment received. *Mantra* and its meaning are two wings of the aeroplane—both wings are needed to take a flight to far-off shores of eternity.

"Speak to Him thou for He hears, and
spirit with spirit can meet...
Closer is He than breathing and nearer
than hands and feet."

—Tennyson

* * *

"He alone, O beloved, is our friend
who goeth with us to the other world;
and He on the day of reckoning,
will stand by us as our surety."

—Guru Nanak

* * *

"I will utter your name, sitting alone among the shadows of my silent thoughts.
I will utter it without words, I will utter it without purpose.
For I am like a child that calls its mother a hundred times, glad that it can say "Mother".

—Rabindranath Tagore

Mantra : our most sincere and reliable friend

Mantra Jāp trains and prepares the individual to rely entirely upon the resources of one's own inner self. At the beginning, one may not develop any personal, intellectual or emotional association with it but as it slowly takes hold of us, it becomes our most sincere and reliable friend. Most of our thoughts revolve around it like a whirlpool developing the most intimate relationship with it. Slowly over a period of time as we learn to absorb the secret word into our subconscious mind, it actually affects and influences everything we do, without our being aware of it. The more we tune ourselves to the words, the more they become a living reality for us.

The phenomenal power of the secret melody can be observed in the activities of every *mantra* user. No matter where we are it gives us company. It is difficult to put into words its subtle companionship, we cannot touch it with our hands, we cannot see it with our eyes, yet something that emanates from it mysteriously takes hold of us and can be experienced at all levels of our consciousness.

In our community we have a little group of friends, and within that group we have only two or three very near and dear one's. They are the friends upon whom we can rely in times of difficulty. There are moments in our life when we feel lonely and empty inspite of the presence of friends and relatives. Such moments of loneliness are quite normal for every individual. The moments when all his relationships fail, the individual feels himself sinking into the gulf of utter loneliness. At this juncture he would give up everything he has for the sake of some words of love and compassion. These are the moments when a person feels that his happiness in life has become dependant on other things and other people. At that time, when he turns inside and gets a chance to talk to the indwelling Divinity he feels at peace. The silent conversation with his inner-self brings so much tranquillity and satisfaction that is quite incomparable to anything else in the world. This is so, because this silent conversation connects him back to the source where he belongs. Spiritual friendship is indeed most reliable, very dependable and true. Quiet recitation of *mantra* can help the individual to establish this friendship with the Indweller—this friendship is honest, unconditional and reliable.

My friendship with my *mantra* blossomed magically from the morning of my initiation. I felt for the first time that I had found a friend, whom I had been looking for all my life. Although the way my initiation took place was quite incidental but once I accepted it with willingness and faith, it aroused my total devotion for the *mantra*. I made no further search, the more I relied upon it, the closer I felt its presence. It is indeed a fact that most of us depend upon so many external sources for peace, happiness and security, and totally forget about the source within.

Ever since I was a little girl, I was always afraid of darkness. The fear grew more specially after my surgery. Sometimes it went to the extent that I wouldn't stay alone at home after dark. So many time, when my husband and my son had to go out for shopping in the evening, I would quickly switch on all lights in the house, open all doors and sit outside in front of the house. Often I felt embarrassed. I asked myself what others would think about all this. But I couldn't help it. I understood that most of our fears are due to some previous *samskāras,* which are handed down to us either from our childhood or from some previous life. Swami Dayananda has also written about it: "impressions once formed, leave such indelible marks on us that they don't die easily. They have to be mercilessly driven out."

After I was blessed with the sacred words of my *mantra,* all the fears started fading. Whenever I was alone in the evening, I started reciting the *mantra* and felt much at ease. I felt the presence of the supreme Lord Śrī Kṛṣṇa all around. It has given me a lot of inner strength and slowly I have been able to overcome the fear of ghosts and darkness. At the beginning whenever I was afraid, I consciously reminded myself of the *mantra* but later on, as the practise strengthened, it has become a second nature of mine. I am always reciting in my thoughts, even without my being aware of it.

The sacred *mantra* recited with deep sincerity unlocks the dormant powers of which we are not usually aware. It constantly keeps one connected with the infinite from where flows the enormous inner security and strength. *Mantra* is the verbal form of energy which comes from within. Human being has enormous potentialities and the potentialities remain unknown and unravelled to us. *Mantra* reveals these potentialities. It introduces us to our own essential nature which is pure and unconditional. *Mantra jāp* brings fearlessness in our lives. It makes us confident and secure. Fearlessness is indeed a sign of inner integrity and stability. In my own experience, gone are the nights when I woke up from sleep crying and terrified. Now I feel strong enough to stay alone at night, and also sleep alone in my bedroom. Any time when I feel slightly scared, I start reciting the *mantra*, and the fear evaporates. This indeed is a blessed experience.

I want to emphasize one important fact here, that the real power of *mantra* partially resides in the grace that comes with initiation. I was taught *Gāyatrī Mantra* when I was about two years old, and was told to recite it all the time, especially in moments of fear and insecurity. I did that, and it definitely helped. The words of *Gāyatrī* are: "*...Om bhūr bhuvaḥ swaḥ tat savitur vareṇyaṁ, bhargo devasya dhīmahī dhīyo yo naḥ pracodayāt...*"

Gāyatrī mantra has been always known as the *mahā-mantra* in the *Vedas*. In *Gāyatrī* lies the whole universe. Meditation with the chants of *Gāyatrī* connects one to the throbbing Being who is the essence of life. It is believed that *Gāyatrī* came out of the primordial sound AUM and all the four *Vedas* emanated from *Gāyatrī*. In the *Vedas, Gāyatrī* is known as *Vedamātā*, i.e. the mother of all knowledge and wisdom. The glory of *Gāyatrī* has been described throughout the *Vedic* literature. *Gāyatrī mantra* according to the *Vedic* tradition should be taught as the first lesson to each child of the family. It should be introduced as the first prayer to the youngster. The importance of learning *Gāyatrī mantra* has been highly emphasized at the time of *upanayan saṁskāra*. The recitation of the first three words, namely, *bhūr, bhuvaḥ* and *swaḥ*, connects the individual to all the three levels of consciousness. These three levels are physical, psychological and spiritual. *Bhūr* symbolizes the physical body composed of five elements: earth, water, air, ether and energy. With prayer one asks for complete harmony and support with cosmic forces. The word *bhuvaḥ* stands for thought process as a controller of astral body or the inner nature. *Swa* stands for the indwelling light the Supreme-self. *Gāyatrī Jāp* brings harmony at all the three levels of consciousness. It keeps electrifying thoughts with spiritual power. It purifies thoughts, speech and action.

There are about 24,000 hymns in the four *Vedas*. The essence of these have been combined into twenty-four syllables called *Gāyatrī*. Ātri *rishi* has been the great seer who sang it for the first time in the most melodious tune, since then it has been known as *Gāyatrī*. *Gāyatrī* is also known as *Sāvitrī*. This is the *mantra* which is used for the worship sun-God. The holy scriptures mention that anyone who worships the rising sun with the recitation of *Gāyatrī,* receives special blessings from the Divine. The worshippers of sun usually live a very long life. *Maitri Upaniṣad* describes the glory of *Gāyatrī* in these words "*Gāyatrī* is the splendour, the beauty and glamour of *Sāvitrī*. Let us meditate on *Sāvitrī* with the chanting of its holy words". There are thousands of translations of *Gāyatrī mantra*. In the words of Swami Shivananda, "Let us meditate on God Almighty and His glory Who has created the universe, who is remover of all sins and ignorance. May He enlighten our intellect". The ancient scriptures describe "*Gāyatrī chandasya mātetī*", i.e. *Gāyatrī* is the mother of all the hymns of the *Vedas*. Similarly in the *Devi Bhagavatam,* the glory of *Gayatri* has been described in these words—"*Sarvaesu vedesu bhuthesu ca Gāyatriastu samārcanaḥ Brahmādyopi dhyāyanti Jāpanti ca*" The worship of *Gāyatrī* constitutes the entire essence of all the *Vedas*. Even Brahma himself meditates on *Gāyatrī*. Swami Dayananda Saraswati, a great commentator on the *Vedas,* has given the meaning of *Gāyatrī* in these words "O' omnipotent Lord, Thou are the dearest life breath. Keep us away from evil intentions and physical sufferings. May we have the pure vision in our mind. O' God lead us from darkness to light. May Thy kindness direct our thoughts towards the righteous path. May we surrender all our work to you and attain ultimate emancipation and liberation."

Anand Swamiji in his book entitled *Gāyatrī Mahā Mantra* gives the meaning of *Gāyatrī* : "O Divine power, you are the creator and sustainer of the universe, may we meditate on thy glorious splendour, and offer all our activities to your humble service. Bless us with mental, spiritual and intellectual strength. Give us the ability of total surrender. Please illuminate our mind with thy grace and inspire our spiritual perception".

The great *Gāyatrī mantra* can be used by anyone. It has a highly compact form. It is indeed a powerful and sacred *mantra*. In most cases it does prepare the individual for the advanced spiritual learning. As my respected mother, Mrs. Dayavati has always emphasized that the *Gāyatrī jāp* which I did regularly for many years since my childhood, had prepared my conscious mind for the initiation from my spiritual teacher. It had purified my ego-centric mind and washed some of the impurities. *Gāyatrī jāp* made me receptive to the subtle perception and assimilation of my personal *mantra.* I can't deny the benefit and the blessings of *Gāyatrī mantra* recited in early years of my childhood. Later in life I learnt several *mantras* and prayers from my grandparents and at the Sunday School but none ever worked so efficiently and positively as the holy *Mantra* which I have been given at initiation. The holy words of my *mantra* came to me as *smiritir labdha,* i.e., the revelation and realization of something which has been forgotten. It is the experience of being restored to something well-known and familiar from previous lives. It is being awakened to one's own essential nature. It is the orientation into a new concept of life. The holy *Mantra* has helped me in re-establishing my perennial friendship with the supreme Indweller. It has taught me to rely upon my own resources. It has become my most dependable friend. It has helped me to understand a part of me which had always remained unknown. It is indeed like being born again in the same life-span.

Mantra Jāp keeps us connected with the indwelling Supreme Soul who presides over the entire universe.

So whenever there is a problem, and our mind is clouded with conflicting emotions, instead of fuming and fretting and analysing, just start reciting the sacred *mantra*. This little shift in awareness will provide all the strength and will answer all your questions. With *Mantra Jāp* we come in contact with some intuitive potentialities which guide us consciously and unconsciously.

I have observed that we can control our dreams with the help of *Mantra Jāp*. The contents of our dreams usually come from the subconscious state of our mind. This spontaneous activity goes on unless some conscious changes are made at the deeper level of consciousness. *Mantra Jāp* introduces the consciousness of the presence of God. It introduces a new thought pattern and gradually replaces the old memories with renewed ideas and eventually brings some changes in our dream pattern.

Living in awareness of the supreme Divinity gives us more control over our thinking process and eventually gives us more control over our dream pattern also. Since childhood, I had, from time to time been haunted by nightmares. In my dreams, I used to see flying golden snakes. Sometimes I saw the cemeteries, strange people, floods and very fast trains passing by. These dreams were always full of realistic details. Most of the time I felt caught up in the middle of a stressful situation. This dream pattern started fading slowly after the *Mantra* initiation. When I had bad dreams and was scared, I started reciting my holy *Mantra*. It immediately gave me relief. Now neither I wake up at night nor I am frightened. The objects of my dreams are peaceful and pleasant. I see mountains, valleys, gardens, temples, rivers and the groups of saints singing and chanting in my dream. All of us have heard the story of Jatila as described by Vandana Mataji. She writes, "Jatila was afraid of going to school all along through the woods. One time his mother told him, 'Jatila, you have a brother, Madhusudhana (a name of God). Call him and you will have no fear.' The little boy was convinced that Madhusudhana was indeed his real brother. So whenever he felt frightened in the forest, he called his brother Madhusudhana and the supreme Lord came Himself in the guise of Madhusudhana and escorted the little boy through the woods."

We also know the story of Bhakta Prahlada. His demonic father tried everything within his power to kill the little boy. Prahlada was thrown from the mountain top, he was asked to sit in fire. The young boy always held strong faith in God. He was always confident that if the supreme Lord wanted him to live, no body could kill him or even harm in anyway. He always recited his sacred mantra *"aum namo bhagavate vāsudevāya namaḥ"* and always felt safe and secure.

Many other traditions in the world also emphasize that recitation of the sacred word always helps people. The word repeated with faith and love can dispel all our fears and fill our lives with strength and confidence. This confidence comes from our belief that "I am not alone."

Among all the fears the most common and the dreaded one is the fear of death. Death itself is not really painful, but the fear hangs heavily throughout our life, especially for those who are not spiritually awake.

At the time of death, people usually remember their worldly attachments and pleasures which make the departing time very painful. A person on death bed feels very frustrated and helpless. First of all his vision becomes very weak and everything looks dark, dim, dull and dreary. Slowly the person's speech becomes indistinct and he cannot communicate with others.

Everything around becomes scary and frightening and the person feels lonely. At the time of parting when nobody else can help, our most reliable friend, *mantra,* comes to our rescue and provides security and peace. During the lifetime, when the sacred *mantra* is constantly remembered, it gets absorbed and recorded in the unconscious and becomes deeply embedded in our thoughts. So at the time of death, the words of *mantra* become very active and engage the conscious mind. That is the time when our most reliable friend *mantra* holds our hand and connects us once again to the supreme Lord. So there is no doubt that the person who constantly remembers the Lord's name and stays connected with it in his lifetime, experiences less pain at the time of death.

With constant repetition, *mantra* strengthens our relationship with the inner self. As the relationship with the indwelling Lord strengthens, our relationship with the outer material body becomes weak in due time and the person feels less pain in discarding the body. Most of us find it very painful to leave the body because of our strong identification with the body, relatives and everything else that exists in relation to the body. All of us are familiar with the story of the King Parikṣit as described in the *Bhagvatam*. Just before his death on the 7th day of his constant connectedness to the supreme Lord, Parikṣit told everybody that the curse of Shringi had proved to be a blessing in disguise. He felt himself liberated from all the fears of death and gladly accepted his fate. In the *Geetā* also the supreme Lord confirms this concept in Chapter 8 (12-13):

sarvadvārāṇi saṁyamya mano hṛdi nirudhya ca
mūrdhnyādhāyā'tmanaḥ prāṇam āsthito yogadhāraṇām.
mityekākṣaraṁ brahma vyāharan mām anusmaran
yaḥ prayāti tyajan dehaṁ sa yāti paramāṁ gatim.

—Having closed all the doors of senses and firmly restoring the mind in the heart and the life-breath in the crown of the head, established in the yogic concentration he who utters the single syllable AUM, the Supreme *Brahman* and remembers Me while departing from his body, he certainly attains the Supreme goal.

Srī Kṛṣṇa suggests that the individual should try to withdraw senses from the sense object and direct the attention at the heart centre *anāhat cakra*. *Anāhat cakra* is the focal point of ever vibrating primordial sound of the holy syllable AUM. When the life force becomes integrated, it enters into the cavity of the heart centre, and immediately recognizes the sound of AUM and instantly joins the *nāda*. From this station the person should direct the infused breath with the vibrating sound of AUM upward at the *Ājñā cakra* at the space between the two eyebrows. When the life force withdraws itself from all the other nine gates of the body (two eyes, two ears, mouth, two nasal passages, organs of defecation and reproduction) and moves upwards, it gradually settles between the two eyebrows, and enables the person to infuse the diffused movement into the Supreme Soul. Slowly the body consciousness starts failing and the person becomes more conscious of the indwelling Supreme spirit. Finally, the inner intelligence guides and directs all the life force towards the crown of the head from where it departs from the tenth gate of the body. This is considered to be the yogic way of departing from the body and merging into the Supreme Soul.

An illustration like this has been described in *Kaṭhopaniṣad,* "Puruṣa the Supreme-Self, perpetually abides in the cavity of the heart, almost about the size of an *anguṣṭhā* (thumb). With concentration on the rhythm of breath and vibrations of the holy syllable AUM, the person directs with firmness the life force from the heart as the wind is forced out from a flute.

Out of all the hundred and one arteries of the heart *(shatam caikaca hridayaya nadias)*, there is one which goes towards the crown of the head. The *Matri Upaniṣad* has described it as the *śuṣhumnā* artery which connects the heart to the soft spot at the top of the head. This soft spot at centre of the skull is called *brahma randhra*. This is the tenth gate in the body used by the yogins at the time of departure from the mortal body. This is a doorway to Brahman. When the individual mounts up and leaves from this gate, he merges into the rays of the sun and becomes a part of the Supreme Self. *Tayordhvamaann amrtatvam et* means departing upward from there one attains immortality. When the mind is withdrawn from the senses, and concentrated on the sound of AUM, the embodied-soul breaks up the ties of bondage effortlessly and the departing moment becomes very peaceful. While giving an elaborate description of the technicalities in the *Geetā*, Srī Kṛṣṇa has constantly emphasized upon the word *mamanusmran* which means repeated remembrance of Me with the recitation of the holy syllable AUM.

The saints and the holy men who are spiritually awake believe that the last minute when a person leaves his body plays an important role toward the voyage to the unknown. They always prepare themselves for the departing hour with constant *mantra jāp* and other spiritual austerities. We can indeed validate this truth by observing the death of some sages who depart from this world with transcendental experience. Their faces are calm, peaceful and established in the transcendental Self. On the other hand, if we have a chance to watch the death of ordinary worldly people, we find that their last hour is generally very restless and frustrating. Their facial expressions show helplessness which indicates that they did not prepare themselves for the moment of departure from the world. I remember my grandfather telling us the most painful experience of one of his friend's death. The name of this person was Mahinder Nath. He was a police officer and did spend most of his life-time at work using bad words for criminals and punishing them. At the time of death, my grandfather started reading the holy hymns from the *Vedas* and requested him to pay attention to the prayers. But Mahinder Nath's mind was embedded in his past memories of jail and criminals, so the only words that came out of his lips were the angry words he always used for people in his lifetime. The words of the holy prayers could not wipe out the strong impressions recorded in his unconscious mind. Mahinder Nath's parting time became very painful and pitiable. That was quite a proof for those who stood around him—that no one else can help anybody at the time of transition except whatever one has practised during the lifetime with spiritual awareness. All these subtle observations lead us to believe that *mantra* is indeed our most honest and reliable friend for our lasting communion with God.

There are many people who plan to go into spirituality, when they retire and have more time. They keep on postponing all their lives till the last minute when they suddenly realize, 'Well! That is it.' Human life is a great gift of God and its each moment should be used and utilized with utmost vigilance and care. "*...āj nagada kala udhāra...*" (आज नगद कल उधार) The time is now and today—we know nothing about tomorrow.

The beauty of human life is that it is never too late. We can start our spiritual journey any time, anywhere and at any cross-road of life. The easiest way to start our spiritual journey is to start with *mantra jāp*. It does not require any special preparation. It requires neither means nor money. Anytime, according to our convenience, we can decide to go for it. With *mantra jāp*, life becomes very pleasant and very loving. Love for life blossoms in all respects. Life becomes very peaceful, creative and enjoyable, and the parting time less threatening and painful. As Tagore writes in *Gitanjali:*

"...I was not aware of the moment when I first crossed the threshold of this life,

What was the power that made me open out into this vast mystery like a bud in the forest at midnight!

When in the morning I looked upon the light I felt in a moment that I was no stranger in this world,

that the inscrutable without name and form, had taken me in its arms in the form of my own mother,

even so in death the same unknown will appear as ever known to me and because I love this life, I know I shall love death as well..."

Excellence in the performance of work is the clear reflection of the yogic unity and connectedness to the source of life.

* * * * *

The highest goal of life can be realized when the person is unassailably established in yogic unity and when he himself becomes aware of the truth that he is living in it.

* * * * *

Live in yoga and work through the uninterrupted consciousness of the Supreme is the swadharma of mankind.

* * * * *

Yoga and Mantra Jāp

The most popular word of *Vedic* literature "yoga" has been derived from Sanskrit root word *yuj* which literally means to bind, combine and join together the psychic energies in order to experience a union and communion with the indwelling Supreme-Self. It is an art which helps the individual to bring his scattered thoughts together into a reflective and meditative state of mind in order to comprehend the presence of the Divinity within. Yoga is the unity of the individual-soul (*Jivatma*) with the Supreme-Soul (*Paramatma*). The *yogic* practice helps the individual to accelerate himself to a state of consciousness in which his egoistic individuality is dissolved. It teaches the technique of directing the attention from the gross body to the nerves and the senses; from the senses to the mind and from the mind to the intellect and the Supreme-Self.

Philosophically, Yoga means union with the Supreme-spirit. The ancient scriptures describe *Yogaḥ-cittavṛtta-nirodhaḥ* which means yoga is to control all the mental modifications. It is an art which persuades an incoherent and scattered mind into a reflective and coherent state. The Yoga system was first collated and written down by the sage Pātañjali in his *Yoga Sutra*. This text consists of one hundred and ninety-five *sutras*. These Sutras are divided into four chapters. The first chapter deals with the theory of Yoga; the second chapter describes the art of Yoga and initiation into practice. The third illustrates the method of comprehending the inherent powers, and the fourth deals with inner unity and freedom from identification with the physical body. The *Yoga Sutra* of Pātañjali also describes the eight steps of self-discipline. These steps prepare the individual for the ultimate experience of union and communion with the Supreme-Self. Yoga practice is not only a means to a certain end, it is indeed both the means and the end.

The eight steps of *yogic* discipline are *yama, niyama, āsana, praṇāyāma, pratyāhāra, dhārṇā, dhyāna* and *samādhi.* For example, the practice of *yama* stands for collective, universal and moral commandments like non-violence, truth, continence and non-stealing. The practice of these *mahavratas* in daily life accelerates and purifies the day-to-day emotions of the individual towards the pursuit of higher goals in life. The *rishi* gave them the name of *mahavrata*. These are considered mandatory for any advancement in personal and spiritual upliftment. *Yama* includes non-violence, truth, continence and non-stealing. Non-violence has been given a great importance in our scriptures. "*Ahinsā parmo dharmaḥ*" (अहिंसा परमो धर्मः)—Non-violence is Dharma of mankind. Ahinsa means "*mansā vācaya karmaṇā*" (मनसा वाच्य कर्मणा)—Never hurt anybody by thought, word and deed.

About the power and the strength of speaking truth I have given a detailed description in a previous chapter. The habit of speaking truth gives one enormous strength. It makes us fearless and confident. It boosts up our self-esteem, which makes us feel very special in our own thoughts. As described in *Mandukya Upaniṣad,* "The Supreme Soul is always attainable by truth, austerity, inner wisdom and celibacy. Sages whose desires and passions have disappeared, who are pure and illuminated in their heart do experience His presence from moment to moment." *Brahmacharya,* i.e. continence, should be observed at all stages of life. It helps one to develop a sound mind and a sound body. It is indeed a doorway to a decent and respectable life-style.

Niyamas are for self-purification such as purity of body and mind, control of desires and the regular study of the holy books. These disciplines train the mind and give inner tranquillity. Next comes *asanas* which are physical exercises. These are important for keeping the body in good shape. *Asanas* are some exercises to build the body and also to keep in tune for spiritual realization. Physical exercises purify the body and also help the individual to eliminate harmful toxins from the body. Physical exercises do help the mind and also the nervous system. These integrate our thought pattern and help the mind, body and inner-self to work in unison.

The next step in *Yogasutra* is *pranayama*. *Pranayama* means conscious control of breath. It is an act of rhythmic inhalation, retention and exhalation. In order to attain mastery in *yogic* communion, *pranayama* plays a significant role. It is the art of breathing which helps the aspirant to monitor his quality, quantity and direction of thoughts. For good physical health and mental health it is very important to do *praṇāyāma* regularly everyday.

Pratyahara means a conscious control of senses. It brings a shift in awareness. It helps one to withdraw senses from the sense objects and leads the aspirant towards introspection. It helps the senses and the mind to search the real happiness within.

The next steps are *dhāraṇā*, *dhyāna* and *samādhi*. *Dhāraṇā* is one-point concentration with faith and determination. It integrates the thinking faculty and slowly leads one to *dhyāna* (one-point concentration). In the state of *dhyāna* the aspirant stays aware of the body, breath and mind. He watches all the activities of mind at various levels. Slowly the outer consciousness starts fading, leading him to infinite tranquillity—a blissful state of total peace. *Samadhi* is the state of mind—very hard to describe in words. It is something which can be only understood by the individual's personal experience.

In *Bhagawad Geetā* Śrī Kṛṣṇa declares the concept of *yoga* as to be in perennial unity with the Divine. It brings inner strength and unity consciousness. It helps the thinking faculty to get settled in the Divine and makes the mind very resolute and determined. Śrī Kṛṣṇa assures that even the highest achievement of transcendental unity is possible through the unity in *Yoga,* because in this discipline the individual works in constant unity with the Divine. The person becomes determined and resolute. Since he works with integral wisdom and stability, the results of his work are unparalleled. A yogi works wonders because of his inner peace and one-pointedness of intellect. The unity in *Yoga* opens the door of inner intelligence to intuitive knowledge and to transcendental experience of the Supreme-soul. The constant practice of yogic unity in the performance of actions enables the person to discover his sublime centre of ever luminous consciousness within his own self. When he becomes settled in that field of awareness, the concept of unity becomes his abiding heritage under all circumstances. It is a well known fact that the highest goal of life can be realized when the person is unassailably established in yogic unity and when he himself becomes aware of the truth that he is living in it.

Mantra yoga means to develop an union and communion with God by constant repetition of *Mantra*. *Mantra Jāp* can be very useful and beneficial in the accomplishment of all the preliminary and preparatory steps discussed for yogic communion. The observance of all the *mahāvrtas* and other disciplinary acts just comes as second nature to a disciple who has been initiated into *Mantra Jāp*. Initiation awakens the dormant energy and *Mantra Jāp* channelizes it harmoniously and systematically. When energy is in harmony, the performance of ethical codes and rituals becomes easy. *Mantra Jāp* tunes the energy for positive goals.

I observe in my life that *Mantra Jāp* has helped me not only in the observation and performance of *mahāvrtas* but in all the spiritual disciplines required for yogic contemplation. For example, speaking of truth, forgiving others, control of desires, observance of *brahamacharya*—all these seemed so challenging and so difficult only a few years ago. But now with *Mantra Jāp* nothing seems impossible. Although bragging about these accomplishments is not good but in my case I honestly feel that it is all due to the Divine grace. I want to share my experiences with others so that the others can get benefit from it and start their voyage with full faith, confidence and without hesitation. The Divine grace is for everybody, and is given when the aspirant requests for it. The communion with the indwelling Divinity, which was just a fantasy and a dream in the past, is a reality for me. The presence of God is felt naturally and effortlessly. To quote Oliver Wendell Holme, "Man's mind once stretched to a new idea, never goes back to its original dimensions."

When the individual starts *Mantra Jāp,* right after

the initiation, his mind becomes conscious of the sound and words of *Mantra*. But the very thought of *Mantra* brings with it the form and shape of the revered Guru. Some disciples are instructed to start *Jāp* by meditating on the Guru's picture. The disciple tries to see the absolute reality in Guru, who is the source of all secret knowledge. The form and shape of the revered Guru is called *Dharmakāyā* in some schools of yogic contemplation. *Dharmakāyā* means the body in which the Guru and the Supreme-Lord reside as one inseparable entity. Slowly the vision of the revered Guru starts fading and is replaced by the formless awareness in *Mantra* contemplation. *Mantra Jāp* is a training of the mind to settle down in *Yoga*. We often find it difficult to meditate upon a word without a thought form which comes with it. For example, we cannot repeat the word flower without its form in our thoughts. So whatever word we utter it immediately brings some form, some idea to us.

It is important to start *Mantra Jāp* with the help of some shape and form of God suiting the individual's temperament. According to Swami Chinmayananda, "Every *Mantra* has a presiding Deity or Devata. The belief is that when one recites the *Mantra* keeping in mind the form of the Deity—then like one being called by one's own name answers to it rapidly." So this way the Devatā is invoked easily.

It is a fact that in spiritual pursuit, as the worshipper advances from less awareness to increased awareness, the 'One' being worshipped also changes, till the individual reaches the shrine within his ownself. It is very difficult to draw a line between the worship of *saguna* and the meditation on *nirguna*. In the process of worshipping *saguna* (God with form), the person actually meditates upon *nirguna* (God without form), who hides behind the *saguna*. So by being devoted to either is indeed worshipping both at the same time. The Supreme Divinity and his manifestations cannot be separated. It is after performing the worship of *saguna* for many years, that the individual educates himself to live in the consciousness of *nirguna* and rises to the 'ideal' behind the 'idol'. For example, in some states of India, especially Maharashtra and Bengal, there is a *visarjana* ceremony which forms the culmination of worship. Around *Navaratra* time people worship various forms of gods and goddesses made of clay. After the worship for nine days all the deities are taken in a procession to the Ganga or to the nearby sea-coast for *visarjana*. *Visarjana* means giving away the concept of forms and names. It is like rising above the concept of *saguna* to that of *nirguna,* from idol to ideal, from less awareness to increased awareness. In the process of worship for ten days the individual is expected to understand the transitory nature of form and move up to the reality of formless.

It is believed that in the course of spiritual progress, an inspired devotee is blessed with the first hand experience of holy communion in due course of time. In the words of Dr. Radhakrishnan: "once you realize that the Reality is something to be felt, something to be experienced, you do not attach much importance to the method by which you attain it. They become subordinate and merely instrumental". People give different names to God in the process of their spiritual pursuit. The form of approach differs from one individual to another depending upon his own personal level of understanding. That's why Srī Rāmakṛṣṇa used to say that it is just enough to have faith in God. For there are several names of God and there are several methods through which one approaches the Divine.

One should not argue that only his faith is right and the rest are wrong. The crescents, the crosses and symbols are only visual aids for strengthening spiritual concepts. The ancient religious literature states that "*Sādhakānām hitārthāya brāhmaṇo rūpakalpanā*". This means that the Supreme Brahman is formless. An aspirant gives name and form according to his own imagination. The *Sruti Bhagawati* declares: "*ekam sadviprā bahudhā vadanti*", i.e. there is only one Truth but people state that there are many. "*Ākāsāt patitaṁ toyaṁ yathā gacchati sāgaraṁ, sarva deva namaskārā Kesavaṁ pratigacchati*" i.e., worship the Lord in any form you like and address Him by any name which pleases you but it is indeed directed to one and the only Supreme Lord. Absolute Truth is indeed beyond the reach of sensory perception. It is formless, nameless, and inexplicable. So either the person has to transcend the finite to experience the infinite or to bring the infinite to the level of finite perception in some form and shape. At the beginning people definitely need some kind of expression to experience inexplicable in order to concentrate during their spiritual pursuit.

Once I delivered a lecture in Moraga High School. The several questions were put before me by the young children but the question which I liked the most was about the founder of Hindu Religion. I was really impressed, and answered that the Hindu religion as is usually known should be actually called as *sanātan Vedic dharma* which originated along with the creation. *Veda* literally means knowledge of the Self, and *dharma* is that which upholds and keeps us connected with it. So *Vedic* religion is as old as the creation itself.

The Supreme Spirit and the primordial Nature both are beginningless. They are both *sanatan*. It is hard to determine the exact date when the world came into existence. As Gurubāṇi says, "*Pitā kā janam kyā jāne pūta, sagala piroi apne sūta*" (पिता का जन्म क्या जाने पूत, सगल पिरोई अपने सूत). *Shrimad Bhagawad Geetā* also explains the similar concept, "*na rupam asye ha tatho palabhyate na nto na ca dir na ca sampratistha.*" Since the entire creation came into manifestation with the union of God and mother Nature, both God and primordial Nature existed before the man appeared. As the man's intellect developed, he became very busy in exploring nature. In search of material comforts as the ancient man moved from one place to another he felt himself caught in the web of pleasure and pain, good and evil, and the things transitory in nature. When he needed help he turned inward and found the comfort in the Supreme-Self. With this inward journey to the self and to the inner-most Self, the ancient man developed the concept of God and *swadharma*. *Swa* means the indwelling light and *dharma* means which upholds or keeps connected.

The voice of the indwelling-Self taught the ancient man the ethical codes, notions of vice and virtue, *pāp* and *punya*, morality and immorality. In connections with the higher Self the ancient *rishis* and sages developed some lines of ethical discipline for people to live in harmony with nature, with others, and with their own self. This code of ethics were given the name Religion or *swadharma*. As I said earlier, religion, i.e. religion, means to go back to the lineage—the lineage which is the indwelling light, *Paramātamā* and *Puruṣottama*. Similarly, *swadharma;* which combines two words—*Swa* & *Dharma*. *Swa* means indwelling light—*dharma* means to uphold. So *Vedic* religion—the knowledge of the Supreme Lord is as *sanatan* as *jiva* and *prākṛti*. All of them developed at the same time. *Vedic* religion is the religion of mankind. The God of an American or the God of a Jew or the God of an Indian cannot be different. All of us belong to the same source as the *Vedas* describe, "*ekam sad vipra bahudhā vadaṅti*" (one God called by different names).

Vedic religion indeed developed with the evolution of man. The contents of the *Vedas* are *Śrūtis*. *Śrūti* existed throughout eternity in the form of sound. Those sounds were heard by our *rishis* in deep contemplation. The words were formed from the sounds and written in the form of *mantras* and hymns. The authors intentionally did not mention their names while writing *Vedas* and other scriptures. Those great seers could foresee the future and did not want to limit the use of *Vedic* knowledge. There are some theologians who consider Āryans to be the founders of *Vedic* religion. But that is not true. The contents of the *Vedas* are the mixed hymns of Dravidians (the original people of South India) as well as Aryans along with some reflections of Greek mythology.

According to some ancient philosophers the knowledge of the *Vedas* flourished in Indian continent. Our *rishis* who came with the inner visions of spiritual knowledge of the *Vedas* and *Upaniṣads* were both Aryans and Dravidians. Both of them lived in Indian continent, whose boundaries, stretched from the southern tip of Ceylon (Śrī Lanka) to farther north-west. *Vedas* literally means knowledge of the Self and *Upaniṣads* means to 'sit close'. The knowledge of

Upaniṣads helps the individual to get closer to the Supreme indwelling spirit.

Since the *Vedic* knowledge developed and took its form and shape in the Indus Valley, it is known as Hindu religion. What is popularly called Hindu religion should be called *sanātan Vedic religion.* By giving it a name, such as Hindu religion, we limit its vast horizon. It is like enclosing the vast ocean into limited boundaries. We can safely say that there was no particular person as the founder of *sanātana Vedic* religion. It developed along with development of mankind and its civilization. It has evolved over thousands of years. *Vedic* religion is the knowledge of the Self, the voice of the Self, the words of the Supreme-Self. *Śrūtis* are the truths which originated from Eternal Truth, the *sanātan* Truth. The *Vedas* are revelations. *Vedic* knowledge is not the prerogative of the people of India only. It belongs to the entire mankind, meant for the welfare of the entire universe. This is the reason why *Vedic* knowledge attracted scholars from all over the world. Max Muller was the first German who translated *Ṛgveda*. Paul Daussen, a great philologist and philosopher of Germany, visited India in 1914. When he was leaving the Bombay harbour he told in his address, "You Indians have a great heritage, cling to it."

Vedic knowledge has inspired people to attain the spiritual knowledge. Muslims and Christians from all around have paid their respect to these vast treasures of Divine knowledge. Schopenhauer used to read some *mantras* from the *Vedas* and *Upaniṣads* every night before going to bed. The elder brother of Aurangzeb, Dara Shikoh was so much impressed by the contents of *Upaniṣads* that he learnt Sanskrit and got the *Upaniṣads* translated into Persian language. *Shrimad Bhagawad Geetā,* the song of the Lord is a highly revered book around the world. This is the only religious book on which the maximum commentaries have been written so far by renowned scholars of the world. In *Vedic* religion one can find the source of many other religions of the world.

At initial stages of *Mantra Yoga Sādhanā* the disciple is advised to concentrate on the favourite attributes of God to stabilize thoughts. When the mind of the disciple is concentrated on the form, the disciple should allow the mental form to fade away. A *Mantra* cannot produce its full effect upon the deepest level of our consciousness if the mind is attached to form and shape. So it is suggested to rise above form and shape and concentrate between the two eyebrows. The spot is known as *Ajna cakra*. Concentration on *Ajna cakra,* with the help of *Mantra,* opens up the third eye. The third eye is an eye of knowledge and intuition.

Intuitive knowledge and understanding plays a significant role in getting full benefit of *Mantra Jāp* in yoga discipline. Rishi Pātañjali has mentioned various stages of intuitive knowledge which the aspirants wish to attain. These stages are described as *taraka, viveka jñāna, pratibhā, prajñā* and *ṛtaṁbharā*. All these are steps from less intuitive ability to increased intuitive ability. People who are highly intuitive have actually developed this particular branch of integral wisdom. It just happens, without being consciously aware of it. Knowingly or unknowingly they live in the spirit of Divine and are consequently able to develop this particular branch of intuitive knowledge. They are very bright, sharp, intelligent and knowledgeable.

Intuition, according to our sages, is inner wisdom, inner guidance, inner awakening. It helps the individual to establish his proper place in the inner world and also in the material world. It gives one the discriminating ability to decide what is right and what is wrong. Sometime it brings astonishing changes in the individual's attitude and can really change his whole course of life. Whenever there is an honest desire for inner change and transformation, the person gets it somehow. The power that controls inner feelings and thoughts guides him to the right path. The Supreme Divinity appears in the form of saints and God-realized souls. They by mere words, can awaken the intuitive knowledge.

In the life story of Swami Dayananda Saraswati, it is mentioned that once Swamiji visited a city in Jhelum. A Satsang was organized every night. During his stay Swamiji noticed that a person used to come daily and sang some devotional *bhajans*. One day Swamiji inquired about this person and found out that his name was Amichand. Swamiji's followers told him that Amichand was not a good person. He drank a lot and his morals were also low. No matter what people told Swamiji about the character of Amichand, Swamiji could still see the later's earnest desire for a change. Swamiji didn't pay any attention to his past life. He just noticed, what the devoted aspirant needed at that time. Next day Swamiji praised his *bhajans* highly and commented , "*Amichand tuma ho to hīrā, para pare ho kīcar me*" (अमीचंद तुम हो तो हीरा, पर पड़े हो कीचड़ में). He said

"Amichand you are a diamond but are lying in dirt and mud". The words of Swamiji touched the heart of Amichand and from there he started his spiritual journey. Amichand stopped drinking and controlled his other bad habits. As his devotion for God strengthened his songs became more and more melodious. He wrote the most beautiful devotional *bhajans*. I remember one line where he writes, *"Jai jai pitā parmānanda dātā……amī rasa pilāo meri ātmā ko, rahūn sarvadā teri kīrti ko gātā"* (जय जय पिता परम आनन्द दाता...........अमी रस पिलाओ मेरी आत्मा को, रहूँ सर्वदा तेरी कीर्ति को गाता).

Any spontaneous change that happens in a personality is directly related to inner enlightenment. It is inner wisdom that guides the individual in the right direction, it is inner wisdom that makes one receptive to the words of the learned, it is inner wisdom that forces one to surrender and tear off all the boundaries of ego. It is through intuition that we come in contact with people who are already on the path of enlightenment. As a great prophet once said, "the healer of all thy difficulties and complexities is the remembrance of Me." The intuition, called the *ṛtambhara buddhi* as our *Rishis* called it, develops only by staying in touch with God—by our connection with

God, by our yogic communion and union with God. This task of yogic unity can be well accomplished by constant recitation of the holy *Mantra*. It is perhaps the best method designed to cater to the needs of the busy modern man.

Mantra Jāp is the greatest source of inspiration in yoga discipline. Grehard Oberhammer describes the use of *Mantra* in yogic meditation in his following words: "In contemplation the *Mantra* is the only reality that is clearly delimited and set in a certain point of time. Therefore, it alone is capable of transforming the mythic meditation of transcendence, immanent to it into an event." *Mantra Jāp* works dynamically, provided the individual learns to recite with love and devotion. When *Mantra* takes hold of the individual, remembering Lord's name regularly becomes a habit. It helps the person to be aware of the Lord's existence all the time. The underlying idea of the *Mantra* becomes fixed in the deeper layers of individual's mind. When *Mantra* recitation becomes a state of mind, then all other methods of *yoga* discipline merely become shadows. This is called *yoga* with *Mantra Jāp,* because it keeps the person's union with God alive from moment to moment. The sound and words become like background music going on with every breath. It becomes an absolutely effortless method of developing an unity consciousness. At this stage of spiritual progress it becomes very easy to go into *Samādhi.* The one-point concentration which usually takes hours in general *yoga* session, with *Mantra Jāp* it comes within the first few minutes of meditation. With constant recitation of *Mantra* our entire thinking process gets charged with God consciousness and going into *Samadhi* comes without much struggle. So we can say that the training by which the turbulent, roaring waves of mind can be compelled to behave into pleasant and peaceful rhythms of tranquillity is constant *Mantra Jāp.*

"The most distant course
comes nearest to thyself, and that
training is the most intricate which
leads to the utter simplicity of a tune.
The traveller has to knock at every
alien door to come to his own, and one
has to wander through all the outer
worlds to reach the innermost shrine
at the end.
My eyes strayed far and wide before I
shut them and said 'Here art thou!
The question and the cry 'Oh, where?'
melt into tears of a thousand streams
and deluge the world with the flood of
the assurance 'I am!'"

—Gitanjali, Rabindranath Tagore

Mantra and the Modern Man

Freedom rests, and always will, on individual responsibility, individual integrity, individual effort, individual courage, and individual religious faith.

—*Apples of Gold*

Modern man lives in an age of "Hurry, Curry and Worry". He has mixed ambitions arising from different angels. For example, occasionally our bank statements give us a warning not to buy big houses. It warns us "You don't need it, You cannot afford it" But on the other hand social pressures cry-out, "No, go for it". The inner voice keeps telling to donate some part of your time and money for the welfare of others but the greed in us keeps postponing all the good work; the Greed claims, "This wealth is mine, I should enjoy it".

Our whole life seems to be entangled in a bundle of contradictions. The ideals we cherish and the realities of life such as comforts of living with modern facilities, our gadgets, ostentation, possessions, pride on materialistic enjoyments etc., all result in conflicts with our ideals. Most of us actually do not lead the kind of lives which we think we should. Quite often, the modern busy man perceives all kinds of signals for his restlessness. He knows that the kind of life he is living is wrong but he can not escape from it. He knows what is right way of living but he does not have the strength to live up to it. This inner conflict is making us weak and almost incapable of solving the very basic problems of our daily life.

Everywhere distortion of values, restlessness of mind and decline in moral standards can be seen. We notice in our modern, progressive and commercially flourishing societies that most of us are lonely. We live a confused, bewildered and unhappy life. A man is indeed a paradoxical being. When a man comes to this world he cherishes two strong desires. He wants to enjoy everything in the world. The nature invites him for it. He wants to drink, eat, acquire and possess every possible thing in the world. But in the middle of all these material enjoyments, some voice from inside keeps telling him—"Go back, where you belong to". So in the midst of all the worldly enjoyments each and everyone of us lives with tension, worries which make life unhappy. Hard pressed, we inquire: "Who am I, why I am here in this world". In that state of mind, we think of God and like to seek His blessings. Further, some of us look inwards for our soul's comfort, and are usually amazed by the silence peace and tranquillity it can render.

Swami Vivekanand has stated, "Each soul is potentially divine". Our soul being a fragment of the cosmic soul can rise to the status of the Supreme-Self, and can actually work in a copartnership with God. In one's lifetime every person can rise to the height of a genius and can become the glory of the world. But if he ignores the voice of the inner-Self and drifts away from *swadharma* he can fall in to the depths of degradation. A man can be the splendour and majesty of the world but also its ridicule. As the Supreme Lord Himself tells in the *Geetā* Chapter (6) 5:

"...Uddhared atmana' tmanam
na 'tmanam avasadayet
atmai 'va hy atmano bandhur
atmai 'va ripur atmanah..."

Let a man lift himself by his ownself; let him not degrade himself, for he himself is his own friend and he himself is his own enemy.

The goal of this life is to manifest divinity from

within and to live in harmony with others and with our own inner Self. This task can be well accomplished by living in constant remembrance of God. In the words of Dr. Paul Brunton, "The Divinity within us, the overself, is always there even when we disbelieve in it and its presence is the secret why sooner or later there must be a an attraction in human life towards spiritual values. Only after we realize vividly human insufficiency and inadequacy are we likely to turn towards it for help, sustenance and strength." The demand of the modern age is spiritual awareness and awakening at the individual level. The outer crisis is a reflection of our inner conflicts. Every individual has to take personal responsibility of going through ethical discipline and inculcation of moral values. It is a task to be accomplished at individual level, by conscious endeavour. We have to realize our dignity as human beings and seek for some solution, for some orderliness and harmony.

It is to step out of a peculiar or particular life-frame which we have created around us. It is a shift in our thinking process which actually enlightens our life style and we start seeing life from a totally different perspective. As Emerson said, "A man is what he thinks all day long. How could he possibly be anything else." Marcus Aurelius, a great philosopher who ruled Roman Empire, has also said, "Our life is what our thoughts make it".

We are a reflection of our thoughts. It is our attitude towards everything and everybody which mirrors our state of mind. It is our thinking process which is reflected in our overall personality. All our choices, likes and dislikes, are the products of our mind.

Billions of thoughts go through our mind every day and influence our behaviour. Every word we speak, every act we perform, clearly reflects who we are. Each thought seems to be connected with some other, and sometime to a series of unbroken parts. All our actions do correspond to our thinking process, our *sanskaras*—our attitude and the state of mind. So if we consciously make some positive changes in our thinking process, we can really change our total life style and our overall personality.

As Omar Khyyam has said, *"I sent my soul to the invisible for some letter of that after-life to spell, by and by, my soul came back to me and murmured in my ears, you! Yourself are heaven and hell"*. It is the spiritual thinking which elevates each individual to the higher levels in life; and spiritual awareness dawns in life by staying in touch with the spirit—the ever-awake Being. God is the innermost being of one's ownself, wrapped up, in so many covers or layers. To get in touch with that indwelling spirit is possible by vigorous discipline of mind which is cultivated with the help of *Mantra Jāp*. The repetition of the holy *mantra* brings a new direction, gives a new flavour to our life. Transformation can be seen at all levels and slowly a new person is born, the type of person we always wanted to be. It brings back our true nature which is fearless, confident, compassionate, kind, and lovable.

Mantra Jāp is the most convenient, most fulfilling and most rewarding form of God worship, specially suited to the busy schedule of the modern man. People quite often say that they want a change in their life style, but they don't know where to look for. They want to worship God, They want to have an intimate relationship with God but they don't have time. As a matter of fact our great sages have been always well acquainted with human weaknesses, so they have described many alternative methods for God-realization and Self-realization. In *Mahābhārata* the sage Vyāsa has said: *Karte yaddhyāyato viṣṇu tretāyām yajña to mukhī dwāpare paricaryāyām kaliyuge tadakirtināt.* This means that the spiritual growth which an individual obtained through meditation in *Satyuga,* through *yajña* and dedication in *Tretayuga,* through worship and devotion in *Dvapara yuga* can be attained and accomplished in *Kaliyuga* by simply reciting the name of the Divine.

In this respect it is worthwhile to quote Swami Brahmananda: *"Jāpam—Jāpam—Jāpam.* Wherever you are and whatever you are doing, let the quiet *Mantra Jāp* go on and on. Keep the divine name churning in the heart while being engaged in your activities. It brings peace and tranquillity. It makes one free from all the insecurities and frustrations. Have strong faith in God and His name".

The holy *Mantra* which is the name of the Lord, keeps calling God no matter where we are and what we are doing. It keeps us connected to the source where we belong and so guides our path through all the ups and downs of life. It gives us company everywhere and then over a period of time becomes our most reliable honest friend.

As we observe most of us are so lonely in life. Why? Because we don't know how to make friends.

The reason we are enable to make friends, because we don't trust anybody else and are not friendly with our ownselves. As Maslow writes, "Americans need so many more therapists than the rest of the world, because they just don't know how to be intimate—that they have no intimate friendship, by comparison with Europeans and others. Therefore they really have no deep friends to unburden themselves to." I personally feel that this is not so only in America but all round the world. Amidst all the material comforts, luxuries, social get-togethers, workshops and conferences, picnics, and beach parties, each individual is lonely, sad, restless, and unhappy. Most of us are really unstable. We need a sedative to sleep and need a cup of tea, coffee or some other stimulant to get up from our beds. Due to the social pressures, both the husband and wife are busy making money. The kids are dragged from the bed at 5 A.M., handed over some breakfast in the car, left at the day-care before the day breaks, and are picked from there at sunset. At the dinner table, everybody is tired and cranky. People usually watch T.V. while eating their dinner and later, everybody goes to bed. Nobody has time for themselves or anybody else in the family.

Our whole stereotyped life-style shows as if we are

trying to prove something to others. Jealousy, greed, and peer pressure is increasing in our societies. Desire for one thing leads to desire for another and as we keep adding things to the chain of our insatiable ambitions, we slowly but surely start feeling trapped. The more a person runs after material comforts, the more he is isolated from his inner-Self. The more we ignore the voice of the inner-Self, the more we are separated from God who gives us strength and protection. As our *Upaniṣads* say, *"Not by means of wealth can a man fulfil himself. He requires other dimensions which he has to develop, and that is spiritual self."* He has to learn to develop an intimate relationship with the Supreme self. It is our separation from the Self which is the cause of our loneliness, our smallness and of course our unhappiness.

Unless we know who we are, and what do we want, nobody can really help us. As Peggy Riley writes, "I don't know who I am." How many bartenders and psychiatrists have stifled yawns on hearing that popular threnody for the thousandth time ! What such people really feel about themselves is to be timid, lonely, colourless, or to be in some way fault-ridden." Similarly, I am reminded of lines from Bertrand Russell's essay,

The Unhappy American Way. He writes, "In the course of my various travels in America, I have been impaired by a kind of fundamental malaise which seems to be fairly common and which poses a difficult problem for the social reformer. Most social reformers have held the opinion that if poverty were abolished and there were no economic insecurities, the millennium would have arrived. But when I look at the faces of people in opulent cars, whether in your country or mine, I do not see that look of radiant happiness which the aforesaid social reformers had led me to expect. In nine out of ten cases, I see instead a look of boredom and discontent and an almost frantic longing for something that might tickle the jaded palate."

This is what we call spiritual poverty and a lack of spiritual intimacy. It is this spiritual poverty that has led millions of people around the world into deep frustration and have forced people even to give up their lives. A similar experience has also been described by Dr. Radhakrishanan when he was visiting U.S. in early sixties. He writes, "During my visit to United States of America, a few young men and women came upto me and asked me, 'what is wrong with us?' I said if you insist me to tell you the truth, it is that when your

Founding Fathers came to this country, they had abundant faith and a pioneering spirit which enabled them to develop amazing economic prosperity. There is a danger that in this material prosperity, you are slowly losing the faith."

Loss of faith in God leads to loss of faith in our ownself which in turn is the cause of our low self-esteem, low self-respect and lack of self-confidence. As Willian James has written, "Faith is one of the forces by which men live, the total absence of it means collapse." One of the reasons for the downfall of any community, any country or any race is the fall in moral standards. The happiness which is preferred over ethics is definitely another form of misery. The fall in moral standards is due to loss of self-respect and loss of faith in the Supreme Self. When people lose their touch with themselves, they lose their touch with everybody and everything else around. It may sound puzzling but this is the truth. When we are at ease with ourselves we are at ease with others also. When we love and respect ourselves we feel like loving others too. It is a good understanding and appreciation of the Self which allows for a friendly and respectful relationship with others. As Deepak Chopra writes, "Whenever we extend a bond of friendship towards others, we actually duplicate the one we have with ourselves." At the deeper levels of consciousness, we are all united and bound by one inseparable thread—the God in us. As Lord Kṛṣṇa writes in the *Geetā* Chapter 7 (7),

"mattah paratāram na nyat kimcid asti dhanamjaya
mayi sarvam idam protam sutre manigana eva"

—which means like clusters of yarn-beads formed by knots on a thread, there is nothing else besides Me, O'Arjuna, This whole creation is threaded on Me. This is indeed true that when we rise above the material body the material world and the egocentric thoughts—we see God in us and we see the God in the entire creation. When a person feels connected with the indwelling Self, the love, respect, kindness and genuine care for the entire humanity shows in anything he does. All his actions correspond to the global well-being. The ideals of an awakened person are supportive of universal life. A person with close friendly spiritual relationship with the Supreme-Self is the one who is able to develop a comfortable relationship with the entire world, which includes all creatures, human beings and the entire environment. That is why our sages have said all along that a person's inner state of mind can be judged by the manifestation of his attitude towards himself and to everything and everybody else around.

The mass disaster which we see around us manifests the inner feeling of man. It shows we have lost respect for almost everything around us. As we observe in our educated and so-called cultured societies, most of us are self-centred and selfish. We create tons and tons of garbage without realizing where would it go. For example, in America the disposal of garbage is becoming a real problem. They are using pressurized deep injection wells at some places, to dump the waste but they don't realize that by using this particular method they are contaminating water for the coming generations. But who cares ! We pollute lakes, waterways and air all around us. We cut more trees than we plant. It is so because we have lost touch with ourselves, we have also lost touch with mother nature—the primordial mother who has taken care of us for thousands of years.

Earlier there used to be one car per family and everybody shared it. People cared for each other. But now in our egocentric societies Me and Mine is becoming powerful. It has made our lives isolated and confined to ourselves. We have lost the ability to share and to live in harmony with others. Most of us are angry, mad and frustrated most of the time. Since we don't care for ourselves, how can we care for others. The question may arise why we are being so insensitive to everything and everybody around. The answer is simple. We have lost our contact with our finer instincts. We have forgotten that our survival and development on this planet completely depends on how we transact with other fellow beings, and how we relate to the rest of the environment. The verses in the *Geetā* and *Upaniṣads* have emphasized about living in harmony. The Supreme Lord says in the *Geetā "parasparam bhavyanta paramvapsyayth"*—fostering one another disinterestedly, you will attain the highest good.

When we live in harmony with nature and take care of everything around us, we in return get full support of nature. This is what has been called *swadharma* in our ancient scriptures. *Swadharma* is to live by the voice of the indwelling Self, the God in us. *Swadharma* is the unique system of values determined by our inner Self. It guides us to perform our duties by keeping in mind the welfare of others. In the words of Swami Prabhudananda, "*Swadharma* is an inner awakening in man which guides him to do what is right and checks him from doing that is wrong."

It demands the expansion of one's identity with the entire universe. As Śrī Tulsidas writes in the *Rāmāyaṇa*, *"Siyaram mai sab jag jani"* (सियाराम मैं सब जग जानी).

All of us are fragments of the Divine irrespective of the caste, creed and nationality. Any type of dealing we undertake, project we handle or advancement we propose, it should be in consideration with the global peace and harmony. As Dr. Radhakrishnan writes, "We must never forget that humanity is not a mere organization. It is a living organism united within by those values which are inseparable from man's dignity and freedom. We break this invisible bond and the body of humanity, if we do not see ourselves present in others."

With constant *Mantra* recitation we can learn to make some contacts with the God in us and can learn to develop a loving and caring relationship with others. We can live with love and compassion within communities and countries. This goal can be well accomplished by regaining our perspective and realizing our unity with God which comes with slow and steady practice of *Mantra Jāp*.

The concept of *swadharma* insists upon treating others the way we would like to be treated by them.

We can treat others with love and respect only if we are able to love and respect ourselves. The latter is possible only if we love and respect the God in us. That is possible only if we give ourselves a chance to know the God in us. And we can experience the God in us, feel his presence in us and communicate with HIM only if we can develop a loving, intimate relationship with God in us.

The close relationship with God can be developed with prayers and *bhajans,* but more so by regularly repeating His name *(Jāp),* by keeping Him enclosed in the deep layers of our consciousness. God exists for those who make an effort to establish a bond with HIM and make the thought of God a living reality, a personal experience. It is true of any relationship. Suppose we have a cousin in France and our father once told about her. Although we have seen her picture but unless we make an effort to establish some contact with that cousin through telephone, letters or a visit to France, the relationship does not exist. Similarly, God is also there but unless we make some effort to communicate with Him through yogic unity or through experiencing His presence, He does not exist for us.

In spiritual journey choosing the right path can be

tough, confusing and frustrating. Everyday we come across with the people from different faiths and beliefs. It is good to listen to others and evaluate each idea. About choosing the right teacher or Guru, I would suggest that one should follow one's own intuition. As Josph Campbell said, "By following your own Bliss you will soon find out, whether you are on the beam or off the beam". There is something inside every individual which guides and brings the Guru and his aspirant close to each other. There is a myth which goes around about the Guru-disciple relationship. Some people think that after the initiation in to a *Mantra,* the person is committed to serve the Guru for the rest of his life. It is believed that the disciple is expected to live close to his Guru and is expected to do all the work his Guru decides for him to do. This is not so. Generally the teacher initiates his disciple and departs away. The relationship between a teacher and his disciple is far beyond the above mentioned relationship. It is purely spiritual and the relationship is at the subconscious level. The Guru does not care whether he is served by his disciple devotedly or not. All he cares about is the spiritual progress of his disciple. Another myth that prevails around *Mantra Dikṣā* is that after the initiation the disciple is committed to the lineage of the Guru and is expected to support it. People think that after the *Mantra* initiation, probably they have to support the Guru's mission financially for the rest of their life. That is really not true.

Mantra initiation has nothing to do with any of material commitments to a certain organization. Nobody is forced to support a faith. The *Mantra* initiation does not enslave anybody; it rather brings freedom in life. *Mantra* initiation does not compel anyone to serve or support any mission. It is completely a matter of choice. A disciple is absolutely free to choose and chart his pathway. A genuine teacher is only interested with the spiritual growth of his disciple. He tries to convince the disciple about the importance of reciting the *Mantra*. So it is not required to stay with the Guru or support the Guru's mission after the *Mantra* initiation. Just the urge of initiation from a teacher, just a slight surrender of ego from the aspirant brings miraculous results. The most difficult step indeed is the acceptance of the fact that there is need of some help for personal peace and happiness—help for self-unfoldment and self-realization. When the aspirant accepts his emptiness inside, the teacher can perceive it immediately and starts pouring his grace in many ways. After the *Mantra* initiation even if the Guru and the disciple are living thousand of miles apart, there exists constant communication between them.

I have already explained in previous chapters that *Mantra Jāp* can really change our life-style. Constant recitation of *Mantra* occupies our entire thinking process, vibrates in each little wisp of our thoughts and enlightens our mind. The spiritual thoughts bring peace and happiness. A mind settled in the essential nature of the Self becomes very peaceful and radiates inner peace all around. It improves our relationship with other people and with everything around. As James Allen writes, "A man only begins to be a man when he ceases to whine and revile and commences to search for the hidden justice which regulates his life and as he adapts his mind to that regulating factor, he ceases to accuse others as the cause of his condition, but builds himself up in strong and noble thoughts; ceases to kick against circumstances, but begins to use them as aids to his more rapid progress and as a means of discovering the hidden powers and possibilities within himself."

I am often reminded of these words of Emerson—"A political victory, a rise in rents, the recovery from sickness, or the return of a friend etc. can raise your spirits and you think that good days are coming over for you. Don't believe in them. It can never be so permanently. Nothing but you can bring peace to yourself." We have to convince ourselves that the solution to our problems does not lie in the help of others. It is within us and within our reach all the time. Our peace of mind and happiness does not depend on where we are or what we have or who we are in society. Rather, it depends on our thoughts, our attitude, and upon the degree of our spiritual awakening. When we learn the art of quieting the waves of mind with constant *Mantra Jāp,* the mind likes to dwell in the tranquillity of the Self and does not pursue the objects of the world for happiness. At that point the individual becomes settled in a state of perennial happiness, independent of circumstances and environment.

The modern medical science is re-establishing something which was said by Epicurus, a great Greek philosopher of first century A.D. He said that we should be concerned about removing wrong thoughts from our mind rather than removing tumours and abscesses from the body." Human body is a vessel of thoughts and most of our conflicts, diseases and discomforts are the manifestations of our impious, bitter, unhealthy thoughts. Mind and body connection is very strong. Our every little experience is stored in the subconscious and does manifest itself in many ways. We have often noticed how strongly sometimes the stomach reacts to a certain shock or sad news. I have often seen some women suddenly start to menstruate upon hearing a shocking news about their loved ones. In some individuals, the stomach cries in the form of diarrhoea and still others may get a heart attack upon hearing a sudden sad news. In describing the role of thoughts that give rise to emotions and feelings in human health and their impact on the physical body, Dr. Candace Pert has said: "Molecules of emotions modulate all cellular activity through intercellular communication and provide a plausible mechanism for the role of the mind and emotions in health. So take care what you think." Our thoughts indeed have a very close relationship to our behaviour, attitude, habits and how we relate ourselves with other people. I am fully convinced by my own experience that any type of treatment given for a disease can help the individual only up to a certain point, the rest has to come from his own inner resources. The real cure has to come from the wisdom of his own body—the wisdom which is controlled by our thought pattern.

The Supreme Lord tells Arjuna in the *Geetā,* Chapter (13) 1:

"idam sariram Kaunteya ksetram iti abhidhiyate etad yo vetti tam prahuh ksetrajna iti tadvidah"

which means "This body is a field—the field of thoughts, feelings and emotions. All our thoughts are manifested through our relationship with others and with everything around." Any body who wants to improve his life-style has to improve the quality of his thought pattern, which comes with the spiritual awareness and spiritual awakening. In the words of Dr. Paul Brunton, "The divine power is not absent from the world nor from any situation which can develop in the world."

If we want this world to be retrieved, the most important thing is to go back to where we belong. Take refuge in thy Self. That's what the word Religion means, 'Re' means 'to go back' and 'legion' means 'to the source'. Any sacred word or prayer or message that links us back to our indwelling Self is religion. We have to learn the method of cleansing ourselves with the help of *Mantra Jāp* and connect ourselves back to our source. This reminds me of a prayer written by Swami Parmananda, "Through the grace of the Supreme Being may I realize that I am a part of the infinitude. May I always act in harmony with His Will."

Our happiness in life depends upon opening such mediums of communication. When we are at peace and harmony within ourselves we are in peace and harmony with other people too. We feel less threatened, less jealous, and less fearful of others. Our relationship improves with our relatives, friends, neighbours and the community at large.

The undisputed fact remains that any kind of transformation in society, awakening for well being, progress, peace and happiness in any community has to start at the individual level. It has to come from the observance of individual ethical codes. Our present sufferings are due to the lapses from the great virtues and values which our parents, grandparents and their parents cherished for a long time.

As the things stand at present, there is a gap which separates us from the Supreme. As soon as we will fill this gap with *Mantra* recitation we can fill the difference. Touch the pulse of that throbbing being who is waiting to be acknowledged by us, who is waiting to be called by His holy name. Hold His hand and then see the treasures of the world— happiness, peace and fulfilment—rushing towards us. I have no illusion that mere repetition of the holy name can actually change our lives. We attend a lot of motivational seminars and listen to sermons at churches, temples and mosques. But accepting the presence of God is one thing and assimilating the consciousness of God is quite another. The consciousness of the presence of the Divine penetrates our mind with slow, constant and regular *Mantra Jāp*. When *Mantra* gets assimilated in our thoughts, it manifests its beauty. Sometimes the change is not visible to ourselves but others can see it. It definitely takes place over a period of time. Some people become impatient for the rewards right after the initiation into the holy *Mantra*. But we must remember that the harder we try to see the rewards, the farther we move away from the essentiality of the *Mantra*. Just make a habit of *Mantra* recitation. Give *Mantra* a chance to become absorbed into the deepest layers of the mind and the transformation will take place automatically. In the beginning it is very subtle but gradually it becomes evident to everybody. As we change, the whole world changes with us, as we change our thinking process we can see changes in others too. *Mantra* recitation reflects the nature of God through us and through others.

Hari Aum Tatsat

Hari Aum Tatsat

Hari Aum Tatsat

Aum Śāntiḥ—Śāntiḥ—Śāntiḥ

ओं पूर्णमदः पूर्णमिदं पूर्णात् पूर्णमुदच्यते।
पूर्णस्य पूर्णमादाय पूर्णमेवावशिष्यते।।

Aum pūrṇamadaḥ pūrṇamidam pūrṇāta pūrṇamudachyate, *Pūrṇasya pūrṇamādāya pūrṇamevāvaśiṣyate.*

पूर्ण अदः	—	That is whole वह पूर्ण है।
पूर्ण इदम्	—	This is whole यह भी पूर्ण है।
पूर्णात् पूर्ण उदच्यते	—	Whole comes out of whole पूर्ण से पूर्ण प्रकट होता है।
पूर्णस्य पूर्ण आदाय	—	Even when the whole comes out of the whole पूर्ण से पूर्ण निकालने से भी
पूर्ण एव अवशिष्यते	—	What is left behind is also the whole पूर्ण ही शेष रहता है।

Everything in the macrocosm as well as the microcosm declares the wholeness of the Supreme-Soul.

A seed becomes a tree and generates thousands of seeds. Each seed from the tree is complete in itself and has the potential to become a tree again. Similarly in our body when one cell splits into two nothing is lost; each cell is complete in itself.

The universe emerges out of wholeness, it is sustained by the wholeness and into wholeness it goes back again.

Excerpts from the book

- The sound energy of the holy syllable AUM is indeed a connecting link to the Cosmos as well as to the deepest mysteries of the Supreme-Self.
- Mantras are a great gift of God to mankind, which came with the creation. Mantras have been designed for the welfare of mankind. They are meant to connect us back to the Creator to whom we belong, the voice of the Supreme-Self.
- Mantra Jāp is meant to uplift the life of an aspirant from the lower levels of ego-centric self to the loftier heights of the Universal Self.
- Mantra recitation is like printing impressions of certain spiritual words into the deepest layers of our consciousness.
- As the heart sings effortlessly the words of the Mantra, we feel as if the whole universe is singing with us. At this point, Mantra becomes endowed with enormous spiritual power, and as it circulates and vibrates throughout the whole body, It energizes each and every cell in the body. All the impurities

are washed out and there comes a boundless love and devotion for God.

- A mind settled in the essential nature of the Self becomes very peaceful and radiates inner peace all around.
- Mukti or Moksha is not only at departure from the world. Liberation and Absolute Bliss can be achieved in one's present life-time and also in the life hereafter. Freedom is living in the awareness of the Divine, freedom is the acceptance of the self; freedom is living a life free from worldly desires, freedom is living in the nature of Supreme Soul.
- We cannot meditate on God just by learning the techniques and technicalities of meditation. The most important factor which enables the meditator to be at ease, is his constant association with God every minute of day-to-day life.
- Liberation and emancipation is to rise above the dualities and conflicting emotions of life. A liberated individual is happy, contented and enlightened. He has the ability to peel away the unpleasant past and holds the courage to live with the situation at hand.

INDEX

A

E

F

G

H

I

J

K

L

M

N

O

P

R

S

T